Dedication

We dedicate this book to you, the ambitious career woman, the driven entrepreneur, the striving sales professional or consultant, whether you are an experienced leader or are just beginning to lead. You recognize the power of knowing what to do, as well as how and when to do it in order to be wildly successful. We salute you for wanting more knowledge designed to advance your business and your career— and we celebrate your commitment to being the best you can be!

The Co-Authors of *Savvy Leadership Strategies for Women*

THRIVE Publishing

A Division of PowerDynamics Publishing, Inc.
San Francisco, California
www.thrivebooks.com

ISBN: 978-0-9829419-8-0

Library of Congress Control Number: 2011930914

Printed in the United States of America on acid-free paper.

URL Disclaimer
All Internet addresses provided in this book were valid at press time.
However, due to the dynamic nature of the Internet, some addresses
may have changed or sites may have changed or ceased to exist since
publication. While the co-authors and publisher regret any inconvenience
this may cause readers, no responsibility for any such changes can be
accepted by either the co-authors or the publisher.

Savvy *Leadership Strategies* for Women

Top Experts Share How
To Take the Lead and Achieve

THRIVE
PUBLISHING™

Table of Contents

Acknowledgements

Gratitude is an important part of business success. Before we share our wisdom and experience with you, we have a few people to thank for turning our vision for this book into a reality.

This book is the brilliant concept of Caterina Rando, the founder of Thrive Publishing™ and a respected business speaker and strategist. Working closely with many of us over the years, Caterina realized how much she was learning about succeeding in business and how much others could benefit from that knowledge. The result was putting our ideas into a comprehensive book. Without Caterina's "take action" spirit, her positive attitude and her commitment to excellence, you would not be reading this book, of which we are all so proud.

Additionally, all of our efforts were supported by a truly dedicated team who worked diligently to put together the best possible book for you. We are grateful for everyone's stellar contribution.

To Patricia Haddock, whose experience in copywriting and copy-editing proved invaluable, and whose magic pen and expertise ensured that this book would be the best it could be.

To Ruth Schwartz, with her many years of experience and wisdom, who served as an ongoing guide throughout the project, your support to our fine production team and to all of the co-authors is deeply appreciated.

To Tammy Tribble and Barbara McDonald, our designers extraordinaire, who brought their creative talents to the cover and book layout, thank you both for your enthusiasm, problem solving and attention to detail throughout this project.

To our exceptional proofreaders, Tony Lloyd and Rua Necaise, thank you for ensuring we dotted all the i's, crossed all the t's and placed every comma where it belongs.

We also acknowledge each other for delivering outstanding information, guidance and advice to you. Through our work in this book and with our clients, we are truly committed to enhancing the success of business women throughout the world. We are truly grateful that we get to do work that we love and contribute to so many in the process. We do not take our good fortune lightly. We are clear in our mission—to make a genuine contribution to you, the reader. Thank you for granting us this extraordinary opportunity.

The Co-Authors of *Savvy Leadership Strategies for Women*

Introduction

Congratulations! You have opened an incredible resource, packed with great ideas that will enhance your business in ways you cannot yet imagine. You are about to discover how to strengthen and develop your leadership skills.

Your business success comes as the result of more than talent, commitment and hard work. Your success will also be determined by how well you lead others to succeed, how productively and effectively you run your business, and how well you communicate and develop employees who deliver stellar customer service that keeps people returning to your business.

We know you want to be the absolute best leader you can be. With this book, you will quickly learn how successful business people get the very best results. As top experts in each of our respective specialties, we have joined to give you the most powerful information and strategies available.

Each of us has seen how even small changes can transform and uplift our businesses. Here is just a sample of the benefits you will find inside:

- Learn how to listen to and trust information from your intuition and senses in addition to your reasoning mind.
- Understand how to coach and mentor others to help them develop their own leadership skills.

• Manage your health and vitality for maximum performance.

• And much more.

All the business professionals you will meet in this book want you to succeed in business and in life. We have outlined for you our top strategies and included the most expert advice we have to advance your success.

To get the most out of *Savvy Leadership Strategies for Women*, we recommend you read it once, cover to cover, then go back and follow the advice that applies to you in the chapters most relevant to your current situation. Every improvement you make will increase your confidence and effectiveness and positively affect how others respond to your business.

Just learning what to do will not create transformation. Take action and apply the strategies, tips and tactics we share in these pages, and you will reap many rewards. With our knowledge and your action, we are confident that, like our thousands of satisfied clients, you too will benefit from these *savvy leadership strategies for women*.

To your unlimited success!

The Co-Authors of *Savvy Leadership Strategies for Women*

Awaken the Leader in You

How to Clarify, Communicate and Bring Your Vision to Life

By Carla Wellington

What do you think of when you read the word, "vision"?

What if I asked you to take a moment—right now—and jot down two or three thoughts that come to mind? Go ahead, try it! Take just a few minutes and write down your initial thoughts when you read the word, "vision." Try not to overanalyze or think too hard about it.

Okay, great!

Some of you may have written down many thoughts and ideas, finding it difficult to stop. Others may have struggled to come up with just one idea or thought. Not to worry. The exercise was meant to help you see how powerful and often used the word "vision" is, and yet how difficult it can be to describe and define its meaning succinctly—especially as it pertains to you and your life as a leader.

Oh, I'm sorry, what was that? You say, "I'm not a leader." Well, whether or not you see yourself as a leader—the fact is, you were born to lead!

Born to Lead

Every person was born to lead in one or more areas of their life—be it in their family life, their work life, their volunteer or charitable life, their social life or their spiritual life. I will focus on your work or professional life, which can include both for-profit, nonprofit, private and government environments.

> *"You were born to lead . . . as heads of communities, companies and even nations . . . [and] nowhere is leadership more crucial than in the family."*
> —Sheri L. Dew, American author and publisher, member of the Commission on the Status of Women at the United Nations

Whether or not you have a formal title or all the "right" credentials and training does not determine if you are a leader. While these things are important when it comes to leadership effectiveness, they do not determine whether or not you are capable of being a leader. Leadership is dependent upon your willingness to fully embrace and use—to the best of your ability—your gifts, talents and influence in service to others with courage, humility and perseverance.

I have met many degreed people who were at a loss when it came to their leadership vision. One such example is of a woman who became a doctor and realized how miserable she was. It was not until she realized her passion was creating art in the form of unique and beautiful pottery that she discovered her professional leadership vision. By following her heart's desires and dreams, she awakened her true vision—what she was born to do.

I have also met many people without formal education who exhibited an amazing, natural talent for leadership in the professional realm.

You too were born to lead and create something only you can uniquely do—with all your gifts, your talents, your personality, your experiences and your strengths—bringing all of it to bear, creating beauty, joy, hope and purpose in your life and in the lives of others.

The Purpose of Vision

"It's a terrible thing to see and have no vision."
—Helen Keller, American author, political activist and lecturer

What exactly is a vision and why is it so important? First, you must realize that every person, every woman, every leader who ever accomplished anything of great value started with a vision. Second, a vision is different from a vision statement. The vision itself always comes first, either as a small, almost imperceptible desire or as a frustration that, over time, crescendos into a palpable unavoidable passion. It might come in a quiet moment of reflection, in an epiphany or from a revelation that shows up unexpectedly and out of nowhere. A vision statement, on the other hand, is how you clarify and begin to communicate your vision to the world.

A vision is a powerful and compelling desire of what "could be"—a picture in your mind's eye and heart of what could be achieved in the future, usually in response to an observed need in yourself and those around you.

The essence of a vision is propelled by a sense of urgency and passion, both of which are powerful motivators that drive ordinary people to accomplish things of extraordinary purpose and meaning in their lives and in the lives of others. In my opinion, there are two women who, more than most, have exhibited and lived their purposeful and obstacle-overcoming visions with great passion and perseverance—Helen Keller and Joni Eareckson Tada.

At the tender age of nineteen months, Helen Keller almost died from a severe illness that rendered her deaf and blind. Through the dedication and support of others, she overcame what many saw as insurmountable obstacles to become one of the most well-known authors, speakers, activists and philanthropists, inspiring many—

young and old, poor and wealthy, sick and healthy alike. You could say her vision was birthed from a passion and desire to show the world—especially those suffering from similar disabilities—that you can do anything you set your mind to as long as you keep your "picture of your desirable future"—your vision—in front of you.

The same can be said of Joni Eareckson Tada, who at the age of seventeen, dove into a lake, broke her neck and instantly became paralyzed from the shoulders down. In spite of overwhelming pain—physical, mental and emotional—she managed to become an accomplished painter, painting with her mouth, as well as a writer, singer and internationally-renowned speaker. No doubt, the vision she saw for herself and others like her was not one of someone who was confined to a bed or wheelchair. Rather, her vision was one that compelled her to overcome every disability to accomplish what she saw and believed was a desirable and achievable future for herself—and to be a role model for others.

Overcoming vision killers. Like Helen Keller and Joni Eareckson Tada, countless other people have found a way to overcome the vision killers of physical disability and pain. There are other less dramatic, yet no less deadly, vision killers. They include naysaying, stereotypes, fear of ridicule, self-doubt, people-pleasing, self-sabotage, fear of failing (or actual failure), tradition, fatigue, burnout, short-term thinking, poor planning, discouragement, complacency and so on. Every leader in pursuit of his or her vision has encountered one or more of these vision killers. I certainly have on many occasions, and you will too if you haven't already.

An important question to ask yourself is, "When a vision killer comes my way, will I give up, slack off, or push through to bring my vision to fruition?"

I hope you find the inner strength, resources and support system to push through and not give up. This chapter will help you do just that!

Why Is Vision So Important?

Well, the answer is pretty straightforward and matter-of-fact:

> *"Where there is no vision, the people perish."*
> —Proverbs 29:18, *The Holy Bible, King James Version*

Without a vision of a desirable and achievable future in a key area of your life, such as family, professional, charity and so on, something inside of you can die and leave you feeling like an empty shell—directionless and without focus or purpose. This often extends outward like a ripple, affecting the lives of those around you. What if Helen Keller or Joni Eareckson Tada had just given up on their vision? Countless individuals and organizations across generations and continents would have missed the contributions of their unique gifts and the inspiration they brought to bear in the lives of those they touched.

This is why your vision is so important!

It is bigger than you are and meant for more than you. Ultimately, it is meant to serve others and make a positive impact in this world.

Clarifying Your Vision

Once you understand the purpose of a vision—what it is and why it is so important—you are ready to start clarifying your vision. This involves two major steps: taking inventory of yourself and writing your vision statement.

Taking inventory of yourself. If you are just beginning the journey of discovering your vision in your professional life, one of the best ways to start is by writing out answers to the following questions:

• What do you do naturally, without much effort? What are your gifts and talents?

- What moves you deeply to compassion and passion?

- What societal problems and issues cause "righteous anger" in you?

- What dream or idea do you have that just will not go away?

- What comes to mind when you think about serving others?

- What do people come to you to help them with?

- What do others say you are good at doing?

- What do you want others to remember about you?

- What would you like to do but are afraid to do?

- What was your most enjoyable job and what made it so enjoyable?

- What have you attempted to do but quit before accomplishing it?

Once you have given adequate thought and time to answering the above questions to the best of your ability, a pattern of common themes, ideas, gifts, talents, strengths, desires and passions will begin to emerge. Often, clients I have coached through this process have had major epiphanies—moments where areas they had been pondering for a while suddenly became crystal clear.

This is the beauty of writing and making things plain. The discipline of writing helps you clearly identify and discover who you are—your gifts, talents, strengths, weaknesses, likes, dislikes, passions and dreams. This, in turn, will help reveal and awaken your unique vision. This flow is depicted in the figure below.

Writing your vision statement. As I mentioned earlier, a vision and a vision statement are *not* the same. They are related, yet distinctly different.

Your vision is a picture in your mind's eye and in your heart of what you could achieve in the future, usually in response to an observed need in yourself or in those around you.

Your vision statement, on the other hand, is a one-sentence, thoughtfully crafted statement that clearly and compellingly describes—in writing—what you see in your vision. It is how you effectively communicate your vision to yourself and to others. Writing your vision statement is the final step in *clarifying* your vision and the first step in *communicating* your vision and *bringing it to life.*

For example, here is what I created for my combined personal and professional vision statement:

"To see individuals and organizations achieving their vision with excellence."

Here are a few good examples of other vision statements that you might find useful:

A nonprofit vision statement: "To see healthy, durable and fulfilling relationships in Latino families."

A small business vision statement: "To create meaningful and effective marketing solutions that increase exposure and sales for local small business owners."

Avon's vision statement: "To be the company that best understands and satisfies the product, service and self-fulfillment needs of women—globally."

What do these vision statements have in common? Each vision statement:

- Describes in a clear and compelling way what the person or organization desires to see happen in the lives of those whom they serve.

- Describes something to be achieved in the future—they are long-term focused.

- Generates emotion and inspires both the owner of the vision and those who read it through the use of powerful language, such as "excellence", "durable", "meaningful", and "self-fulfillment".

- Expresses something bigger and larger than the vision holder.

When creating your leadership vision statement, include these key components:

- Clear and compelling

- Results-oriented

- Long-term and future-focused

- Inspiring and evoking emotion

- Big, hairy, audacious

Once you have created your leadership vision statement, write it down on several 3 x 5 inch cards and post it in as many places as possible. By doing this simple exercise, you keep your vision before you as a constant reminder of what you want to accomplish and "bring to life."

Bringing Your Leadership Vision to Life

"Vision without action is merely a dream. Action without vision just passes the time. Vision with action can change the world."
—Joel A. Barker, American scholar and futurist

Up to this point, you have learned:

- How to awaken your leadership vision by learning why you are born to lead

- The purpose of a vision, what it is and why it is so important

- How to start clarifying your vision by taking personal inventory of your gifts, talents, strengths, passions and dreams

- How to effectively communicate your vision by writing a clear and compelling vision statement

You are now equipped with a foundation to start bringing your vision to life! How do you do this? How do you bring your vision to life?

You need a plan—a roadmap that will get you from where you are to where you want to go, filling in the gaps along the way.

The Awaken Your Vision™ diagram below depicts the key ingredients and steps for developing a plan to accomplish any leadership vision. As you can see, everything flows down from the clarification of the vision. Each section of the plan is supported by and composed of the sections below it.

Awaken Your Vision

Over the next four weeks, I challenge and encourage you to:

• Take your own personal inventory by thoughtfully answering the questions in that section of this chapter. See pages 5 and 6.

• Develop a vision statement for your personal or professional life. If you already have a vision statement for one area, pick another area of your life and write a vision statement for it. Make sure it includes the five key components listed on page 8.

• Based on your vision statement, write three, one-sentence goal statements you will focus on accomplishing in the next three to six months to bring your vision to life.

• For each goal statement, identify three detailed action steps you can take to accomplish your goals.

• Finally, make a list of the resources you will need to start carrying out your vision over the next six months. The two major categories of resources include people and finances, which are further fleshed out in the form of a detailed budget.

"Learn to move toward your goals and desires, one step at a time—often just one baby step at a time—and learn to love the doing. When you multiply tiny pieces of time with small increments of daily effort, you too will find you can accomplish magnificent things. You [will] find you can change the world."
—Jaroldeen Asplund Edwards, American author

As you continue bringing your vision to life, know that it is a process—a lifelong journey filled with many ups and downs. Some days you will not be able to contain the passion that drives your vision. Other days, you will wonder if you will ever be able to overcome vision killers that seem to come out of nowhere. When those days come, and they will, remember the excerpt on page 10 from *The Daffodil Principle* by Jaroldeen Asplund Edwards, published by Shadow Mountain in 2004. Place it where you can see it alongside your vision statement and let it inspire you on your journey.

CARLA WELLINGTON
Business Strategist
Vision Communications Group

Clarify. Communicate. Connect.

(770) 422-1803
carla@visioncommgroup.com
www.visioncommgroup.com

Carla Wellington delivers consulting, training, coaching, meeting facilitation, writing and editing services to for-profit and nonprofit organizations in the areas of leadership development, strategic planning, organizational development, program development, operational improvement and revenue development.

Carla provides her clients with the understanding, confidence and ability to identify, address and overcome the unique business or nonprofit operational and human resource obstacles that they face. She is passionate about helping women identify and use their gifts and talents to create wealth and new residual income streams while building their businesses. She enjoys collaborating with like-minded professionals to help organizations and individuals operate more efficiently and effectively and make the most impact in the lives of their clients, communities and world.

Carla also partners with The LEAD Institute of Atlanta to provide visioneering and strategic planning workshops to local nonprofit organizations. She is a guest speaker and instructor at local and statewide leadership conferences and seminars. Carla recently served as a co-trainer and lead coach for Atlanta's Safehouse Learning Community—a nonprofit program that serves youth, families, homeless and elderly populations.

The Secret to Savvy Leadership
Developing a Strong Inner Core

By Kim Zilliox, MBA, MA, CPCC

What is the secret to being truly respected and followed as a female leader? How can a woman be perceived as strong, approachable and commanding yet not intimidating? These are questions women leaders struggle with. Although more and more women are represented in senior leadership positions, women leaders are still extremely underrepresented across the board.

A savvy leader is strong, confident and grounded. She works well with and inspires others, is strategic, results-focused and manages adversity with grace.

Savvy leaders are not born. They are made through taking risks, learning from mistakes, consistently developing themselves and getting up one more time than they fall down. This chapter will help you on your journey toward becoming the best savvy leader you can be.

Many behaviors are associated with great leadership, and all of them are predicated upon who a leader is at her core. Recall the many leaders you have known throughout your career. Some were great, and some were not so great. What distinguished the great ones?

It probably was not just one thing. Most likely, it was a combination of elements, all stemming from a strong inner core that determined each leader's effectiveness.

What do I mean by *inner core*? Your inner core is your essence. It is what you stand for, who you are and what you believe about yourself and others. It stems from your inner confidence.

The great news is that you can strengthen your inner core, regardless of your starting point. We are all on a lifelong quest to do so. If you are up for the challenge of being the greatest leader you can be, of being a savvy leader, I encourage you to complete each of the exercises in this chapter.

Four Steps to Becoming a Savvy Leader

The following are four fundamental steps I use to help my clients build strong inner cores. I am going to walk you through each one of them. If you do not already have a special notebook in which to write about your leadership development, please get one and use it to jot down thoughts and answers to the exercise questions in this chapter.

Step 1: Believe in Yourself

Step 2: Determine Your Strengths, Manage Your Weaknesses

Step 3: Come from the Right Place

Step 4: Continue to Grow and Develop

Step 1: Believe in Yourself

Believing in yourself is the foundation of a strong inner core. You need to become your own best advocate and your own best champion. You are what you believe. Whatever you tell yourself about yourself is the truth—for yourself.

In your notebook, answer the following questions:

• Do you believe in yourself or is there work to do in this area?

• If there is work to do, where is it needed?

• If you question who you are as a person, what can you do to change that?

• If you have doubts about your leadership skills, what can you do to change that?

This book and this chapter are a great beginning.

• Write out a description of yourself as if you completely believed in yourself.

• Write what you would want someone to say about you at some point in the future.

• Write what you would want to say about yourself at some point in the future.

Do not filter it with what your head is telling you today. Do not worry about anyone else reading it. Just write it with abandon.

Many years ago, I coached a senior vice president for a technology company. The other day she sent an email to me that said, "Kim, I was moving offices over the weekend and opened my binder from the days when you first began coaching me. I can hardly remember who I was back then, but in leafing through my notes, a passage stuck out because I have it underlined, highlighted and starred as I remember your asking me to do. I became incredibly moved when I realized the description written on the page five years ago is exactly who I am today. It immediately brought me back to the very insecure place I was in back then, when I was listening not only to the naysayers around me but to my own negative inner critic. I remember writing it *knowing* it was not true and would never be, but you were so right.

It has absolutely come true and then some. All I had to do was listen to the right voices around me and inside of me. Thank you so very much. —Susan."

Write your own description and suspend any disbelief as Susan did. Let yourself create a vision of your best self in the future. Post this description where you will see it every day, such as on the bathroom mirror, on your phone or on your computer, and read it aloud to yourself each day until you realize it is true.

As Marianne Williamson so eloquently wrote in her book, *A Return to Love,* published by Harper Paperbacks in 1996, "Our deepest fear is not that we are inadequate. Our deepest fear is that we are powerful beyond measure. It is our light, not our darkness that most frightens us. We ask ourselves, who am I to be brilliant, gorgeous, talented, fabulous? Actually, who are you *not* to be?"

Step 2: Determine Your Strengths, Manage Your Weaknesses

"Find something you're passionate about and keep tremendously interested in it."
—Julia Child, American chef and author

Focus on what is right—instead of what is wrong—as a means to personal development. Answer these questions in your notebook:

• What are your natural strengths?

• What do you do extremely well?

• What do you enjoy doing?

• What do people acknowledge you for?

These may be competencies you take for granted without realizing that others may not be as naturally strong as you are in a particular area. If you are like most people, and especially most women, you do not take a step back to review these questions very often.

Remember a time when you were successful in your career. What talents did you use? What are you consistently recognized for? Are there areas you would like to develop further?

Ask others what they think your top strengths are. The following list shows strengths I have found to be most common in the clients and groups with whom I work. They are provided as examples. It is important for you to take time to determine your own individual top strengths:

Responsible	Influential	Proactive	Positive
Visionary	Creative	Decisive	Leadership
Articulate	Driven	Innovative	Thorough
Judgment	Strategic	Intelligent	Collaborative

Take your notebook and let's explore your top strengths. Write down what you believe they are, based on the questions and suggestions above. Include a definition of the strength in your own words.

For each strength, identify at least two ways you can use or develop that strength more. Can you use it more in your current role? Can you help another team? Can you take on a new project? Can you take a course or study more about it?

Here is the most important part of this exercise: Set a goal for developing each strength and calendar it! Take your calendar and create appointments to complete each of these activities—then complete them, because goals without actions are just great ideas.

Manage your weaknesses. If you are weak in a certain area or there is something you want to develop more, it needs to be addressed if you are going to be a successful leader. For example, one of my current client's original goals was to be a strong public speaker. However, she was nervous and uncomfortable speaking in public.

Speaking is an essential skill to develop to achieve career and leadership success, so she needed to become competent in it. After we focused on this area, she grew and developed into a skilled public speaker and now actually enjoys it. This takes effort, and you can do it if you are committed and take action.

Take your notebook and identify three areas holding you back from being the savvy leader you want to be. These are areas that need to be improved at some point in your career, and if improved, would open more doors for you in your chosen field or profession. Now, create two action items for each.

Step 3: Come from the Right Place

When I interview senior leaders in my leadership webinars, most live and work according to a personal mission statement or a vision. I believe both are critical to leadership and life success. If you do not create a goal and a plan for how to reach that goal, you could end up anywhere, including somewhere you do not want to be.

I was recently interviewed in a webinar and shared my mission statement: "To be an amazing leader. To inspire others to act to the best of their ability and achieve the greatest results possible with the highest amount of integrity. To make an incredible difference in the world and to the people around me on a day-to-day basis."

This step is about identifying who you want to be as a leader. Think of great leaders you have known or read about. What were the qualities you admired? What were their strengths, and what did they do to manage areas where they were not as strong?

Take your notebook and keeping these leaders in mind, write a description of the leader you want to be. Here are some questions to help you create your own personal savvy leader description:

• How do you want to be known?

• What do you want people to say about you?

• What impact do you want to have and create?

• How do you *not* want to be?

• What do you admire most in leaders?

• What do you dislike most in leaders?

• What is your personal mission?

• What vision do you have for yourself as a leader?

Compare this description to the one you created in the first exercise about believing in yourself. Are they similar? Post both descriptions together where you will see them, and one day, they will have blended into one overall depiction of who you are at the core.

Step 4: Continue to Grow and Develop

"I do not think that I will ever reach a stage when I will say, 'This is what I believe. Finished.' What I believe is alive . . .
and open to growth."
—Madeleine L'Engle, American writer

A characteristic of a great savvy leader is confidence coupled with humility. This comes from knowing you are in a good place even though you always have an area to develop or improve. Part of developing a strong core is knowing you will always work to be the best leader you want to be.

- Take continuous action toward your goals. Take small steps and, occasionally, large ones. Use Sunday evening or early Monday morning to plan for the week and include some aspect of your leadership you want to develop in the week ahead.

- Schedule time in your calendar for yourself for reflecting, creating, networking, researching, practicing or whatever you need to do to move to the next level of savvy leadership. Honor that time as sacred. If you find yourself giving it up for other, more "urgent" matters, look at what you consider urgent. Part of having a strong core and being a savvy leader is treating yourself with respect and taking care of your needs.

- Finally, celebrate often! Take time on your commute home each day to celebrate what you have accomplished that day. I find that people focus on what they *should* have done differently or on what they did not do. However, with focused, proactive planning and attention on what you did well, you will accomplish more of what really matters. Take time to celebrate victories both great and small. Find three things you did well each day and document them to build up your inner core. Building healthy and honest self-acknowledgement into your daily routine will strengthen your core in no time.

I met with an emerging leader recently at Yahoo!® We had worked together for about four months, and as I described the contents of this chapter to her, she said, "You know that was one of the single, most profound differences I made in my life so quickly. Each night, I have made it a point to write three things in my journal that I have done well for the day. At first, I literally could not write a thing but through our coaching, I have realized I actually do many things well—and a few really well. The act of writing this in my journal every night cements this and provides me with positive messaging. I am so much more confident as a person and as a leader!"

Sheryl Sandberg, COO of Facebook; recently spoke about why a smaller percentage of women than men reach the top of their professions. She encouraged women to be a stand for themselves in the workplace. I passionately encourage you to pursue your career dreams, strongly believe in yourself, know the strengths and gifts you bring to your chosen profession and develop a strong long-term support structure to blossom as the best savvy leader you can be. You can do it!

KIM ZILLIOX, MBA, MA, CPCC
Consultant, Coach, Speaker, Author
KZ Leadership

Inspiring the leader within™

(408) 979-9876
kim@kzleadership.com
www.kzleadership.com

Kim Zilliox specializes in developing the leader within each of her clients to create maximum career satisfaction and contribution. She has coached and developed leaders at all levels for nearly twenty years in the San Francisco Bay Area and beyond. She works with leaders, teams and organizations to achieve the highest results possible in challenging and evolving business environments. Kim brings to her clients a wealth of knowledge about leadership effectiveness, talent development, team building, change management and employee engagement.

Kim's clients cross numerous industries and include: Google®, eBay®, Yahoo!®, Apple®, Oracle®, Disney®, Charles Schwab®, Safeway®, and PG&E®. A sought-after speaker, she has presented at numerous conferences, organizations and academic institutions across the country and leads webinars for senior and emerging leaders through partner affiliations.

Kim earned a master of business administration from the University of California, Irvine, a master of arts in career counseling from Santa Clara University and a bachelor of arts in psychology from University of California, Santa Barbara. She is a Certified Coach®, qualified in the MBTI® and HBDI® and Hogan Instruments®, certified in the Lominger 360® and is an expert in the DiSC® instrument and StrengthsFinder®.

The Leadership Mindset
Transform Your Life from the Inside Out
By Jane Morrison, CLC

At the heart of leadership is the leadership mindset. It puts you in charge of each moment of your life.

The leadership mindset is the driving force of success, propelling you forward to achieve your dreams and your goals. It is an "inside out" process, requiring practice, discipline and wisdom.

At the core of the leadership mindset is the belief you have something of value to offer and that you can make a difference in the world. Believing in yourself and thinking positively takes courage when faced with a difficult or challenging situation. The leadership mindset is a way of thinking that makes a successful outlook more likely to come true.

Henry Ford, founder of Ford Motor Company, sums up the leadership mindset beautifully in the quote: "Whether you believe you can or believe you can't, either way, you're right."

The Leadership Mindset and Women Leaders

I was raised in a generation that rewarded me for being "a good girl," which went hand-in-hand with traits like being agreeable, conciliatory and easy going. On the other hand, my brother could speak his mind and be more opinionated without repercussions.

Unfortunately, it is often assumed that when a woman speaks her mind, she is "being difficult" and may not be liked or accepted. This can be a nightmare for a woman in a leadership role.

> *"No one can make you feel inferior without your consent."*
> —Eleanor Roosevelt, former first lady of the United States

Cultivating the leadership mindset may be more difficult for women who have been discouraged to speak up and find their voice. To those of you who have been silent and in the background too long, know you can develop a leadership mindset that allows you to speak up and have a voice for your needs and wants. See "Leadership Is a Growth Process" by LaNell Silverstein on page 45 for some related information.

What Does Success Really Mean?

Putting a leadership mindset into practice does not necessarily mean you will go into the world, do great deeds and accomplish noble tasks. The leadership mindset is all about doing what is best for yourself and others in the present moment. It is about being in touch with your values and making a difference in the world, in big or small ways, sometimes for yourself, sometimes by influencing the lives of others.

I had been working with Tara for three years as her business and life coach after she opened a home décor boutique in our neighborhood. It was a pleasure seeing her bring together a community of women as she taught them to decorate on a dime. She was doing her life's purpose work and was passionate about it.

After a while, the pressure of running a successful business began to take a toll on Tara. It took her away from her family, her hobbies and other creative projects. She began to feel unfulfilled. The demands of long days in her boutique drained her and made her feel overwhelmed and stressed. Should she close the shop—something she had painstakingly built from the ground up—and spend more time at home and with her family?

Through our personal coaching sessions, she decided it was time to close the business even though she was worried what others would think and might judge her for this decision. However, making the decision to follow her heart did not mean she failed! She was being courageous and making choices that would create new experiences.

Tara used the mindset of a leader, connected with her personal values, stepped up and acted courageously to let some things go that no longer served her. Six weeks later, she was joyfully and blissfully puttering in her garden, making cupcakes with her grandbaby and pursuing creative endeavors she had put on the back burner.

Has there been a time when you have been uncomfortable with your current situation and had to rely on a leadership mindset to make something happen? Did you commit to your decision even though others might not like it? Did you move ahead, hoping for the best positive outcome? This is a leadership mindset in action. See Christina Dyer's chapter, "Everyday Leadership," on page 203 for more on this subject.

Having a leadership mindset means trusting yourself enough to act in your own best interest and the interests of those for whom you are responsible, even though it may not be the popular thing to do.

Here are seven steps for creating and cultivating a leadership mindset. As you read through these steps, I suggest you have a notebook at hand to record your thoughts and answers to some of these questions.

Step One:
Envision a Positive Outcome for Every Situation

The single most important factor of success in any situation is your attitude. My 85-year-old mom is an amazingly resilient woman who always expects the best to happen. It is as if the Universe is listening to her thoughts because more often than not, things go her way. At any unexpected bump in the road of life, she chooses not to see it as an obstacle and does not let anyone or anything rain on her parade.

When you address life as if problems were opportunities, you get stronger, become more resilient and are more adaptable. If you expect the best in any situation, you become an optimist. Adopt a positive attitude on a daily basis and intend positive outcomes. This is a leadership mindset.

When you read these words, *Opportunityisnowhere*, what do you see?

Many people read this as, "Opportunity is nowhere." Some read it as, "Opportunity is now here."

How did you interpret it?

How positive is your attitude? Do you view challenges as opportunities? Remember, what you focus on expands, so choose optimism and, like my mom, you will more than likely get a more positive outcome!

Step Two:
See Leadership Opportunities All Around You

A title does not make someone a leader. What makes you a leader is putting the leadership mindset into action every day under normal circumstances.

Leadership moments are all around you. It takes only a moment to respond to circumstances as a leader. Knowing yourself, your ability to evaluate a situation, to react and to act comes from having a leadership mindset. By taking a deep breath, putting things in perspective and knowing you can make a positive difference, you will demonstrate your courage and integrity as a leader.

The leadership mindset can get you through a difficult time. When my son Shawn was young and his bones were still growing, he suffered from frequent dislocation of the radius bone in the elbow. His elbows dislocated at the joint when he was doing normal kid activities like swinging on the monkey bars or climbing up a tree branch. When this happened, both of us naturally got quite distraught—I sometimes more than he. I would take him to the doctor's office where the doctor would gently maneuver the joint back in place, remind us that he would outgrow this condition, and we would go on our way.

On one occasion, however, we had a new doctor who was not familiar with Shawn's case. He kept attempting to manipulate the arm back into place, which only made things worse. My poor child was in agony. At that moment, I needed a leadership mindset to be an advocate for my child while respecting the attempts of the doctor to make things better.

The situation called for me to have the confidence to stand up for my son and face this medical professional, something most of us rarely do. I pointed out that the situation was not improving. While I respected his attempts, I asked that someone else be brought in who could accomplish what we needed—a quick resolution of Shawn's pain.

This was a fearful situation for me. I had been brought up not to question people in the medical profession. I could have easily lost control and made the situation worse by over-reacting in anger or by not saying anything at all. By taking charge of the situation with a leadership mindset, I got the problem solved.

Step Three:
Eliminate the Negative,
Increase the Positive Influences

Your environment and the people who surround you influence you. In order to remain positive, hopeful and courageous, you must eliminate negative influences and increase positive influences. The books you read and the people you associate with determine where you will be in five years. Where do you want to be?

• Stop reading bad news in the newspaper and watching mindless violence on television, especially just before bedtime. Stories about violence, disasters and so on feed negativity and pessimism. When you sleep, your mind processes the last things to which it was exposed. Do not end your day with negative ideas.

• Spend more time with positive people. Positive associations lead to creativity, partnerships, solutions and better outcomes. Sometimes, when you begin to live your dreams, other people will become jealous and hurtful, and may try to hold you back or even sabotage you.

• Read positive, uplifting publications that keep you focused and motivated. Start reading books about people you admire, personal growth books, books on success principles and books about others who overcame challenges, and you will feel energized and inspired.

• Listen to positive audios and CDs. Use travel, driving and computer time to learn and grow. Fill your brain with inspiring wisdom that helps you develop as a savvy leader.

By acquiring, maintaining and protecting a positive attitude, you will see your success grow and your enjoyment of life improve. You will become more attractive in every way and will increasingly enjoy being around other like-minded people.

"Keep away from people who belittle your ambitions. Small people always do that, but the really great make you feel that you, too, can become great."
—Mark Twain, American author and humorist

Step Four:
Leadership Mindset Is a Way of Life

Incorporating the leadership mindset into your daily practice is necessary for anyone striving to be a leader. My coaching clients share a common trait: When they are learning something new and trying to incorporate a new way of thinking or acting, they get frustrated when they slip up. They become very hard on themselves and believe they have failed.

The leadership mindset is like any other behavior you want to incorporate into your life. It takes practice. Practice means you do something regularly in order to become better at it.

Focusing on what you do not do perfectly increases anxiety and decreases confidence. Instead, focus on the learning and growth process and take pressure off yourself to do something right. If you tend to be a perfectionist, start practicing being kinder and gentler to yourself as you incorporate new changes into your life.

Step Five:
Treat Yourself and Others with Kindness

Your thoughts create your feelings, which create actions. Positive thoughts and feelings propel you forward toward your goals. Negative thoughts create negative feelings that keep you stuck and in a negative, depressed state of mind.

If you want results, you have to have a positive frame of mind. Doubt, fear, insecurity, worry and judgment are ineffective thoughts and feelings that lead to ineffective behaviors and freeze your ability to take effective action. On the other hand, when you practice kind thoughts about yourself and others, you are motivated and can move forward more easily.

Avoid being stuck in victim mode or in blame games. Only one person can create your future and be responsible for your life. That is *you*!

Be aware of what you say to yourself as you go through your day. If you catch yourself engaging in negative self-talk, stop. When a thought saps your confidence, question its validity by asking yourself, "What is the evidence this thought is true?" Usually, there is nothing to support it. When you are feeling down, inadequate or need confidence, remember everything you have accomplished so far in your life. Tell yourself you are an incredible woman and leader. What would your best friend say about you if you asked her to describe you? I am sure she would have a lot of positive praise.

Step Six:
Take Risks, Strive to Learn Something Every Day

When you do something that is outside of your comfort zone, you cannot fail!

You can do well and achieve your goal, or things might not work out. Either way, you can be proud of yourself for trying and learn from your effort. Do not let fear get in the way of trying something new or taking risks.

Being a business owner has been one of the biggest challenges of my life. When I decided to open a coaching and consulting company, I did not know much about owning a business. I was a skilled coach and thought that would be enough. Little did I know I had so much to learn about effective marketing strategies. Just mastering online social media was a major undertaking.

I remind myself that as a leader, I am on a continual learning curve—that I may never feel completely comfortable or finished. I look forward to being a student and learning something new each day. I have to remember to acknowledge myself for what I have accomplished and to not expect myself to be perfect.

When you feel afraid—and even the most successful leaders feel afraid—act just a bit more confident than you feel, and you will actually feel more self-assured. Believe in the value of your skills, your wisdom, your gifts and knowledge, and then share them with others.

Step Seven: Pay It Forward

Think about those wonderful people who influence you positively and help make you more successful. For me, they are colleagues who patiently explain new technology to me, coaches who point out how my way of thinking could be holding me back and good friends who pick me up after a loss. They encourage me to remember my gifts and my own wisdom.

When I first began moving up the ranks of management, my shyness was a detriment. At meetings, I would often defer to others. I had been promoted to a leadership position of power and prestige, yet I had a hard time holding my ground during heated management debates.

I got up my courage and asked to meet with the top person in our department, a woman I greatly admired who was not afraid to speak her mind. She became my mentor, and I learned much about women in leadership roles, about myself and about how to effectively lead. I always remember her advice, "If you've got a song to sing, you've got to learn to sing the tune and sing it loud and proud." She taught me how to find my voice.

Mentors are inspirational leaders who help others make a difference. As a leader, share your positive mindset with others, encouraging them any way you can. Paying it forward is a gift that keeps on giving.

Imagine the Possibilities!

Having a leadership mindset can totally transform your life from the inside out as you begin to see the world as a whole, new place of potential. Gone are the fears and doubts, the "what ifs" and "should haves." Now you have hope, joy and possibilities for a life of fulfillment and delight.

As my client Tara found, saying no to some things means saying yes to something new and wonderful. Make the leadership mindset your way of life and imagine the possibilities!

JANE MORRISON, CLC
Mastering Your Motivation

Empowering you to reach your dreams

(763) 262-6467

jane@janemorrison.com

www.janemorrison.com

www.savvywomenentrepreneurs.com

Jane Morrison is a personal success coach, trainer and speaker with a passion for helping women skyrocket their success to the next level. For more than twenty years, she has focused on combining her love of people with the thrill of helping them reach their full potential as businesswomen and leaders.

Jane believes success in business starts with personal leadership and acquiring the leadership mindset you need to "think big and get into action." She is an expert at helping you create a vision for your future, improve your confidence and overcome hurdles to reach your personal and professional goals. She shares her expertise to help you discover new ways of thinking and maximize your strengths for a joyful and balanced professional life.

The Savvy Women Entrepreneurs' Association, one of Jane's many personal and business development programs, teaches business sales and marketing techniques specifically for women who want to gain the clarity, confidence and consistency they need to charge what they are worth and build a loyal customer base. Through her mentoring, training programs and speaking engagements, she leads individuals and organizations to new levels of success, accomplishment and leadership.

Authentic Leadership and Self-Awareness

Making the Connection—Leadership Lessons I Learned from Mom and Dad

By Terry Barton

I used to have a coffee mug that said, "A female manager's checklist for success: Look like a lady, Act like a man, Work like a dog."

I no longer have the mug. It was long ago misplaced. However, the sentiment has stuck with me. It resonates now as it did then and not for the reason you may think. True, my gender certainly played a role in my own and other's expectations of me, but it did not impact my success. What impacted my success was how I consistently treated people and how I handled situations.

I learned this early on: Successful leaders treat people with respect and equality, are forthright and forthcoming and act in the best interests of the individual, the team and the company, not themselves.

Back in the day, we did not have a name for this. Today, we call it *authentic leadership*. Luckily, I worked with many great leaders who demonstrated this, and I would have to say that the two people I really need to thank for this lesson are my parents.

> *"We're here for a reason. I believe a bit of the reason is to throw little torches out to lead people through the dark."*
> —Whoopi Goldberg, American actress, political activist and talk show host

My brother and I were raised in Boston by wonderful, hard-working parents who taught us how to be good people. They set the example and showed us how to do the right thing, be good neighbors and be true to our word. Both my brother and I have enjoyed long management careers, and as it turns out, our upbringing was a great foundation for our chosen professions. The three leadership lessons my parents taught me are: Do your work graciously, do what you say you are going to do and put yourself in other people's shoes.

We all have opportunities to be authentic and self-aware, whether or not we actually manage a team or have a leadership role. I will use the perspective of someone in a leadership role. Keep in mind that these concepts apply to situations personally and professionally and also for those not in leadership roles.

Let's look at each of the three lessons I learned from my parents.

Lesson One: Do Your Work Graciously

This lesson has to do with taking ownership of your role and being accountable for the outcome.

No matter what your job is, do it fully and completely. There is a concept called "100 percent responsibility," which in business settings, holds that you are 100 percent responsible for the outcome of anything you are working on, regardless of who else might be working on it.

For example, in a team with three team members and a leader, each person has 100 percent responsibility for the outcome of the team. The leader has ultimate responsibility for the team organizationally, but each member has 100 percent responsibility to see that the team is successful, not 25 percent each. If each team member only contributes 25 percent, then the remaining 75 percent is left on the table. In other words, if each person is 100 percent responsible for the success of the team, then there is a total of 400 percent responsibility that is available and should be accounted for.

This particular lesson was hard learned. My brother was responsible for cleaning up the yard—a duty he often shirked. One day my mother asked me to do it. I, angry at my mother for asking me and angry at my brother for not doing his job, proceeded to clean up the yard. I complained the entire time and, frankly, did not do a very good job. Unaware that my mother had witnessed my tantrum, I returned to the house, where she quickly pointed out the error of my ways. Basically, she asked me how many times had I been in the yard that week and if it would have been easier if I had cleaned up the yard one of those days, instead of letting it go. Of course, my response was, "But it's not my job!" She replied, "Yes it is because I asked you to do it."

My brother did get in trouble for not doing his chore, but I am the one who had to write, "I will do my work graciously" 100 times. After that, I cleaned up the yard if it needed it.

There are a couple of points to all of this:

- First, whether or not it was my brother's assigned duty, my mother asked me to complete the task. I needed to complete it and complete it 100 percent.

- Second, I was part of the family team. When I saw that the yard needed to be cleaned, I needed to do it without being told.

To this day, I use the concept of 100 percent responsibility with my teams. While we each need to be accountable for our individual goals and objectives, we all are responsible for the success of the team and need to be willing to jump in, pick up the slack or graciously help each other out. This includes me. As the leader, I need to pitch in as needed.

As leaders, you are certainly familiar with the team member who invokes, as I did, the "It's-not-my-job" rule. You know what this attitude does to the team and the person who holds it. From a team perspective, it can cause animosity and resentment towards the team member. It can mean lost productivity or re-work. If the attitude is displayed outside of your team, it can reflect poorly on you and the entire work group. For the individual, it can mean lost opportunity, strained relationships and a damaged reputation.

There certainly need to be clear roles and responsibilities on a team, and each member needs to be held accountable for their individual role. However, as leaders, you must set the overall tone of working graciously and taking 100 percent responsibility. You must reinforce the concept that everyone on the team is responsible for the success of the team, and each member needs to be willing to jump in as needed. This is a basic expectation I have of all team members. My team meetings include a discussion of what is on each person's plate, who needs help and who can assist. This concept applies to the extended team as well. At extended team meetings with my boss's direct reports, I offer my team's assistance to my peers. Why? Because we are also 100 percent responsible for the success of the extended team. In addition to ensuring that the team is successful, this concept provides team members with opportunities for professional development and exposure beyond a person's job description.

"My grandfather once told me that there are two kinds of people: those who work and those who take the credit. He told me to try to be in the first group; there was less competition there."
—Indira Gandhi, Indian politician and former prime minister of India

Lesson Two:
Do What You Say You Are Going To Do

This lesson is key to being an authentic leader. It is not a hard lesson to grasp. However, it is difficult to practice because it requires that you speak with integrity, make agreements you can keep and strive to always do your best. What makes this difficult are the forces around you that pull you away from these simple tenets.

As a leader, you have competing priorities, meetings to attend and day-to-day responsibilities to be juggled. In the often-chaotic work environment, commitments may get broken simply because you run out of time and bandwidth. You can only handle so much, and when you are over-extended, something has to give.

The real lesson here comes from how you deal with the moments when something has to give. Are you honest? Do you admit your shortcomings? Do you accept responsibility for not keeping your word? Do you recognize what effect your broken commitment may have on the other person?

There are so many examples of how my parents impressed this lesson upon me simply by holding me accountable to the agreement I made to someone. When I started working, it was my responsibility to manage my work schedule. If I did not do that, and one of my commitments had to be broken, I had to talk to the person who was affected. Even if I were sick, my mother would not make the phone call for me. I had to muster my energy to call my manager or my dance teacher to explain why I would not be at work or dance lessons that night. In the case of work, I had to find someone to take my shift before I called my manager. You see, my responsibility did not end at just calling to say I would not be coming in. It extended to solving the problem I created by not coming in.

To put this into practice as a leader, you must lead by example, keep your cool, accept responsibility and communicate openly and honestly. The same is true when you respond to a team member or colleague who has not done what they said they would do.

Lesson Three:
Put Yourself in Other People's Shoes

This is perhaps the most important lesson—to put yourself in someone else's shoes and understand how they feel or why they are reacting or thinking a certain way. It is a valuable skill for leaders because it helps you understand the impact of your leadership on your team members.

My parents expressed this in a simple way: They would ask us, "How would you like it if someone did that to you?" This simple, powerful question forces you to consider your actions and their impact on the other person. In "leadership speak," we call this *reframing*, and it means redefining an issue from a different—often the opposite—perspective. This practice also helps you develop something called *self-awareness*.

> **"Self-awareness: An awareness of one's own personality or individuality."**
> —www.merriam-webster.com

Self-awareness is knowing how you react to certain situations and why you react in a certain way. It takes into account your beliefs, your values and your definition of yourself.

In his body of work, Chris Argyris, a noted thought leader in organizational development, discusses self-awareness as *espoused theory*—what you think you are doing—and *theory in use*—what you actually do. Typically, because of your beliefs, values and definitions of yourself, there is often a gap between what you think you are doing (espoused theory) and what you actually do (theory in use). The goal of self-awareness is to help you bridge that gap and get the two theories closer together. As leaders, being able to close that gap is key to your success. When you are not aware of this, your actions are in opposition to what you think you are doing. This can cause performance issues for yourself and your teams.

I learned this when I was promoted to a senior management role in a division that was going through a reorganization. Priding myself as a collaborative leader who did not micromanage, I handled the situation as I always did. I delegated and allowed my team to take on more responsibility, or so I thought. This was my "espoused theory" based on what I believed. My "theory in use" was quite different.

I was succumbing to the pressure of my new role, micromanaging the team, causing more work for myself and inhibiting productivity. It was not until a brave team member called my attention to this that I realized I was frustrating myself and my team by my actions. Had I just taken a moment to reflect on what was happening, I would have realized my role in the situation and could have taken steps to change it. When I look back on it now, I recall I was tired, frustrated and not thinking too much of my team. In reality, *I was the problem.* I was trying to do everything and not letting my people step up. I did not recognize that the reason I was not getting the results I wanted was because I was acting in a way that was preventing me from doing so. I had not considered my team's point of view.

There are many ways to become more self-aware and understand how and why you react in certain ways. Any 360-degree assessment can provide you with insight into how your team, colleagues and manager perceive you. You can take personality assessments, like DiSC® or Myers-Briggs®, both of which are designed to help you identify your personality type and your preferences for things like your need for information, your communication style, or whether you are introverted or extroverted.

A simple way to get your espoused theory and theories in use closer together is to reflect on what is happening and whether or not the outcome is what you want. If not, chances are you are doing something—or not doing something—that is giving you the result you do not want to get! Ask yourself this question, "What am I doing or not doing, that I need to start doing or stop doing that is giving me this outcome?"

This question puts you in other people's shoes and reframes the situation for yourself. Answering this question forces you to think about what is happening from another perspective in order to see your own personal role in the situation.

> *"Leadership should be born out of the understanding of the needs of those who would be affected by it."*
> —Marian Anderson, American opera singer

To say leadership is a complex business is an understatement. Today's large, highly matrixed, global organizations require technical skills in addition to deft people management ability. The pace of business is so fast, organizations are hard-pressed to keep up, and the people in those organizations are taxed to meet the constant challenges. There is a myriad of leadership theories and self-help philosophies designed to help people navigate the organizational minefield. For me, at the core is authenticity, which requires accountability and self-awareness. Mom and Dad, although they did not know it, taught me how to be an authentic leader.

There is also an element of service to others in these lessons. To do something graciously, do what you say you are going to do and put yourself in other people's shoes means to move the focus from yourself as the leader and to consider the people with whom you interact. Try it. Choose one of these lessons, put it into practice and see what happens. Does your team notice, do you get better results, do you have more productive interactions with others? The answer to these questions may surprise you!

TERRY BARTON

Founder,
TBG Consulting—The Barton Group

(510) 748-9437

terry.barton@thebartongrp.com

www.thebartongrp.com

Terry Barton is an accomplished facilitator, trainer and executive coach with more than twenty years of management and leadership experience in the retail, container shipping and biotech industries. She holds a master's of science degree in management and organizational development from the University of San Francisco and a bachelor of arts degree in speech communications from the University of Maine. She is an adjunct faculty member at Chabot College.

An active member of her community, Terry serves on the board of directors for the Golden Gate Chapter of the American Society of Training and Development® (ASTD) and is vice president of professional development.

A native of Boston, Terry hails from a long line of teachers and coaches. She has seen firsthand that people and organizations get in their own way and prevent themselves from moving forward. Putting that experience to use, she founded TBG Consulting—The Barton Group, a San Francisco Bay Area consulting firm. Using her unique approach, East Coast sensibility and "the single most powerful question anyone could ever ask," Terry helps clients connect to what is preventing them from moving in the direction they want to go.

Leadership Is a Growth Process

By LaNell Silverstein

Defining moments are the moments that make or break you, determining whether you are a true leader.

One of my defining moments came in 2007. The mortgage industry imploded. Banks and lenders across the United States failed. People lost their homes. My role as the San Diego regional manager for a national lender was to be tested. Our corporate office began looking at each regional branch to determine whether it should stay open or not. The pressure was on.

I called my staff into the conference room, and I could see fear in each person's eyes. They looked at me for direction and reassurance to help calm their fears. I looked at each of them with great resolve and said, "We have a choice. We can curl up into the fetal position in the corner and cry like a baby, or we can stand up and take control of the situation by asking ourselves what we need to do, then create a plan and execute it!"

The room was silent. One person stepped forward and said, "What do I need to do?"

Another person did the same and another until everyone had stepped up to the challenge and said, "I'm in!"

We focused on the facts and not on emotion. This helped us put together a strategic plan. We met several times throughout the year to adjust our plan based on what was happening in the market. I am very happy to say we are not only still here, we are prospering and continue to meet regularly to examine and adjust our plan. We are consistently one of the top three branches in the United States and annually fund more than one billion dollars in loans for the San Diego region.

This did not happen by accident.

Leadership is not a skill you are born with—it is a growth process. Like all growth processes, there are strategies you can use to develop your leadership strength. My staff and I called upon many of those strategies during those challenging times of the mortgage meltdown. Now, I am going to share them with you to empower you to develop and hone your leadership skills—skills that will serve you in every area of your life. They will help you lead your staff, your family and any volunteer organization you serve.

"If you want to succeed, you need to learn as much as you can about leadership before you have a leadership position. Good leadership is learned in the trenches."
—John C. Maxwell, American leadership expert, author and speaker

Leaders Never Stop Learning

Successful people have one room in their home that unsuccessful people do not have: a library. If you want to be a leader, you must invest in your education. I am an avid reader and read, on average, a book a week. This is one way I grow personally and professionally.

Reading gives your mind a workout. The more you learn, the more you can achieve. When you put good "stuff" into your head, your mind will grow strong, and you will counteract the effects of any negative messages around you, such as from the media, toxic people and so on. These negative messages will drain your energy and de-motivate you.

Every quarter, I give my staff and sales executives a book to read and ask them to turn in a book report after reading it. The first time I initiated this developmental assignment, I encountered resistance and skepticism and my staff grudgingly went along with it. This attitude has long passed. Now, they eagerly look forward to each book assignment. I am excited when one of my employees tells me how the book she read helped her see things more clearly and inspired her to move forward professionally and personally. Some of the most helpful books I have found are those that condition your mind, reinforce what you know, teach you something new and encourage you to take action.

In addition to reading, attend at least one seminar or training every quarter and purchase the accompanying compact disc and DVD sets. This will allow you to continue the learning process when the program is over. While this can seem expensive, the money you spend will come back to you tenfold. This is an investment in yourself and your leadership skills that will help you maintain a positive focus and strengthen your ability to make decisions and to take action. It will motivate you to keep going when the going gets tough.

Leaders Surround Themselves with Other Leaders

My network is a valuable leadership resource for me. To become a leader, you need to surround yourself with other leaders. By attending seminars and workshops and through networking with other leaders, you will expand your ability to generate dynamic ideas and find better solutions to challenges. Consider joining a mastermind group or hiring a success coach in addition to meeting successful and like-minded people both within and outside your industry who can help you get to where you want to be.

Stay in touch with leaders who are experts on particular subjects, so you can broaden your knowledge. Cultivate these relationships and seek out mentors who can help you on your leadership path.

Be a mentor yourself and share your knowledge and expertise with someone who is striving to achieve what you already have accomplished.

What can you do to expand your network and interact with leaders in your industry and other industries? I belong to two industry-related organizations: the Women's Council of Realtors and the California Association of Mortgage Professionals. I also belong to eWomen Network,™ an organization of entrepreneurs and professional women who bring in trainers and other professionals for monthly meetings. This allows me to network outside my immediate industry.

Leaders Believe They Can Achieve

"Go confidently in the direction of your dreams. Act as though it were impossible to fail."
—Dorothea Brandt, American author

The biggest obstacle many people face on the path to leadership is fear. "What-ifs" cloud their mind. The "what-ifs" undermine your intentions and erode your self-confidence. You begin to doubt yourself and your abilities. You start questioning your decisions and after a while, you become so stuck in the "what-ifs," you are unable to move forward.

Do any of these statements ring true for you?

• What if I succeed, then what?

• What if I cannot handle my new responsibilities?

• What if I fail?

• What if people judge me?

Statements such as these can create strong, negative feelings and come from a belief that leaders were born leaders and that leadership is easy for them. In order to become who you want to be, you must first outgrow who you currently are. Always ask yourself, "Is what I'm about to do taking me closer to the leader I want to be?"

True leadership can only be learned through experience, facing challenges and overcoming obstacles. Leaders confront their fears and stay focused on the desired result. This sets them apart and inspires others to model them. To do this, you must equip yourself with knowledge and insight from the leaders you most admire. You must believe in yourself and your abilities. No matter the challenge, leaders believe they will succeed.

The vice president of my company once drew a big dartboard on a flip chart and said, "We start out at the center. Then we take a few steps out, and when we get too uncomfortable, we take a step back. However, we never go back to where we started."

Challenges are just opportunities to develop the skills needed to become the leader you want to be.

When the "what-ifs" get in the way of your ability to lead, stop and ask yourself, "What is the worst that can happen if I act? What is the worst that can happen if I do not act?" Try to figure out what is behind the "what-ifs" and get to the heart of the matter. Look at areas where you have been successful in the past to bolster your self-confidence. Consult with a trusted colleague or friend and ask for their advice and evaluation of the situation. Every leader suffers the "what-ifs" at some time. However, true leaders do not let them stand in the way of moving forward.

Let this encourage you when the going gets tough because leaders have fears and obstacles to overcome. Leaders confront their fears and stay focused on the result—this sets them apart and inspires other to model them.

Leaders Accept Responsibility and Take Action

Many people have impressive titles and do not demonstrate strong leadership skills. On the other hand, others who do not have titles demonstrate true leadership skills every day. You earn the right to lead others, and this starts with accepting complete responsibility for your thoughts, words and actions. My staff was willing to do just that when we hit that wall in 2007.

While you cannot always control the circumstances around you, you can control how you react to them. Here is the process I used with my staff to create a path through the turmoil of the meltdown. First, answer these questions, and then create a plan.

• What is the problem or challenge you are facing?

• What has contributed to it?

• What is the result you want?

• What action can you take to get the result you desire?

If you do not know what you want, take some time to get quiet and focus on the answers to the above questions. Figure out what *you* really want, what your vision is. Be honest with yourself and start by taking inventory of where you currently are.

• What do you already know and do that will contribute to making your vision a reality?

• What skills and knowledge do you need to gain in order to succeed?

• How can you acquire these skills?

• Whom do you know who has these skills?

Leaders Lead by Example

> *"Being powerful is like being a lady. If you have to tell people you are, you aren't."*
> —Margaret Thatcher, British, former prime minister

As a leader, part of your job is to inspire the people around you to push themselves—and, in turn, the company—to greatness. To do this, you must show them the way by doing it yourself. Becoming a model others can follow is a key leadership skill. It often requires you to stand tall and confident when you are trembling inside! Here are some tools to help you be a model others can follow and emulate.

• Have a vision.

• Model the behavior you want others to emulate.

• Be inclusive.

• Be a good listener.

• Be a good communicator.

• Be consistent.

• Be trustworthy.

• Demonstrate integrity.

• Accept responsibility and accountability for your actions.

• Follow your own rules in the office.

• Keep commitments even when it is inconvenient.

• Embrace change.

• Be open to different ideas and opposing opinions.

• Be an avid learner.

• Genuinely care about other people.

• Praise often and openly.

• Admit mistakes and fix them quickly.

• Stay in the facts and avoid acting or responding from emotion.

• Analyze data quickly and take action.

Leaders Are Resilient

Resilience is the ability to bounce back from obstacles and move forward despite setbacks. Think of the Energizer Bunny®. That rabbit never stops beating its drum, no matter what obstacles it encounters! Resilience is built through trial and error and knowledge of both yourself and what is happening around you. Start by understanding your strengths and areas where you need improvement.

Understand the challenge. Analyze the challenges you face and identify several ways to meet them. Determine what resources you need, what resources you already have and what resources you need to find. Use your leadership network for guidance and assistance with this.

When the mortgage industry hit the wall, my staff and I reviewed the situation we were in and approached it from several directions. We looked at workflows, staff responsibilities, customer service and so on—and we created a plan of action. We continue to have monthly meetings in each department to make sure we are on track and to discuss any improvements or changes needed.

Manage stress. When you are resilient, you handle stress appropriately and even use it to become a stronger leader. Questions to ask yourself include:

• What causes you stress?

• How do you demonstrate stress?

• Do you function well or poorly when you are under stress?

• What can you do to manage stress better?

Look at your answers and the factors in the environment you can control. Strive to maintain physical, mental, emotional and spiritual well-being.

Monitor your impact on others. Be aware of how you are interacting with others, especially your staff. Understand how your actions and attitude affect them and work at maintaining positive interpersonal relationships in order to effectively influence and lead.

My staff trusts me based on past decisions I have made on behalf of the branch. Before making changes in our systems, I get input and feedback from the account executives and internal staff since they are doing the work and utilizing the systems that are put in place. Getting feedback from them helps me make educated decisions. As a result, the branch owns the decision because they were part of the process.

"The challenge of leadership is to be strong, but not rude; be kind, but not weak; be bold, but not a bully; be thoughtful, but not lazy; be humble, but not timid; be proud, but not arrogant; have humor, but without folly."
—Jim Rohn, American author and speaker

Start Cultivating Your Leadership Skills

Take a few minutes to evaluate your leadership strengths and areas for improvement. Find and talk to leaders you admire and want to model. Demonstrate leadership and help others develop their own skills.

Improving your leadership skills is a wise investment of your time and energy. Becoming a great leader is a lifetime process and is reflected in your every action and decision. Regardless of your field or profession, when you improve your leadership skills, you enhance your value in any profession and in all parts of your life.

LANELL SILVERSTEIN
Sierra Pacific Mortgage

Mastering leadership skills for life

(619) 997-2249

lanell@lanellsilverstein.com

www.lanellsilverstein.com

LaNell Silverstein entered the mortgage industry in 1978 and is a driving force in Sierra Pacific Mortgage, one of the nation's Top 25 Tech Savvy Lenders, according to mortgage-technology.com, August 2010. She is a regional manager of the San Diego division, and her branch has been in the top three nationwide for several years.

With her contagious enthusiasm and captivating energy, LaNell is skilled in the art of mentoring individuals to help them become the masters of their own destiny both personally and professionally. She is a designated trainer and advisor, nationally coaching constituents to achieve maximum leadership potential. Her belief in the power of education has led her to take—and teach—many seminars and workshops, and she has earned a certification in behavioral therapy, specializing in clinical hypnotherapy.

LaNell enjoys assisting executives and entrepreneurs in identifying, clarifying and creating a plan to achieve their goals. Through her seminars, training programs and coaching, she demonstrates her unique ability to motivate people to achieve their objectives.

Reinvention with Intention

By Karen Báez

For a leader to become extraordinary, reinvention is required. This is a continual journey that is never mastered, and is well worth taking.

The foundation begins by becoming aware of your current modes of operation, noticing your habits and tendencies and deciding what serves you and what does not. This chapter is about the value of reinvention to you—as the leader of an organization and of your extraordinary life.

Part of reinvention is to first evaluate your core strengths and your weaknesses. Even though they have served you in some way, they may also be limiting you.

• Paying attention to detail can be an excellent quality. However, excessive attention to detail can be a form of procrastination and a means of limiting yourself. When does this get in the way of your growth and development as a leader?

• Being the go-to person can make you appear competent, but when does it hinder you and others? Do you prevent others from stepping up and into their greatness when you continually take control to show them how it's done? What else does this keep you from leading?

- Being known as an easy-going, charismatic leader may work for you, and what does it cost you when you avoid difficult conversations? Are you failing to get your own needs met and are you giving away your power?

What is required for reinvention is an intention to become aware of and to surrender old habits, then generate and practice new ones even when it seems counterintuitive or challenging.

A client came to me with a clear vision of herself as a strong and fearless leader in business. Confidence was her strength and led her to become an award-winning business development consultant and to accept a new position as vice president of sales and marketing.

In a series of 360-degree interviews with her division, she was viewed as brash, impatient and difficult to communicate with. In her view, however, division projects were delayed because her team was not moving fast enough. We took a deeper look into what was really getting in her way, and she made some interesting and life-changing discoveries.

As a child, she had to move a lot and changed schools frequently due to her parents' divorce. She hesitated to mix with her new classmates and held back, finding herself ostracized. When she expressed sadness, her mother admonished her to be brave and not show fear. She developed a strategy to not show her feelings and to force herself to act despite feeling fearful. This had served her well for much of her life, and she had little tolerance for what she perceived as "weakness" in others. Ultimately, this caused conflict with those around her who were reluctant to charge ahead as she did.

This confident, take-action strategy she assumed in childhood had served her well up to this point in her career. Yet it was not going to benefit her going forward. She recognized that if she was to become an effective leader, she had to look within and learn new habits. One of them was to begin to practice compassion. To do this, she needed to show compassion for herself first. She recognized the age-old wisdom—what we cannot tolerate in ourselves, we cannot tolerate in others. Once she realized that showing vulnerability was normal, and not weak, she discovered an effective way to connect with people on a deeper level. Allowing and demonstrating compassion for herself and others was a new way for her to lead.

Her team began to see a shift in her, and she started to notice when she became impatient and less tolerant. Instead of alienating people with her judgments of weakness, she slowed down and asked her team what was missing. What did they need in order to take action? Team communication improved, and people began to see her as more patient and approachable. She reinvented herself as a successful leader of her organization through self-evaluation and a new self-awareness.

> *"If you find it in your heart to care for somebody else,*
> *you will have succeeded."*
> —Maya Angelou, American poet laureate and author

The Fundamentals of Reinvention with Intention

The core components of this process are:

- **Vision.** The imagined future of your intended reinvention should be vivid, inspiring, attainable, measurable and speak to your purpose.

- **Commitment.** The value of your intended vision must be compelling enough for you to stay the course even when challenged.

- **Declaration.** This is a statement of your intention to move it from an idea, a wish or a hope into action. The act of declaring it possible sets things into motion.

Vision

Reinvention with intention requires a clear vision of what you want to reinvent. Take some time and imagine what your life would look like if you knew you could not fail. Write in your journal or paint a compelling picture of what this looks and feels like.

- How will you know when you have accomplished it?

- What measurable result would indicate that you reinvented something in your life?

- What will you gain from it?

- What value will you create for yourself and others?

- Are you passionate about it?

I was walking on the beach with a dear friend, and we started to discuss what we each wanted in the year ahead. I asked her if she had made a decision about becoming a full-time real estate agent in the coming year.

My friend replied that she wasn't sure of her reasons for making this move. She had wanted to be a real estate agent because she believed she should be doing something more with her life. However, she was not passionate about it. She thought it validated her and made her a role model for her daughters.

Our conversation turned to the deeper issue of what she wanted in her heart, and what she would do if she could do anything and not fail or be judged. Her true desire became clear—she wanted to spend as much time as possible with her daughters. She was passionate about being the most present and best mother she was capable of being. She had clarified her vision.

"We are limited, not by our abilities, but by our vision."
—Author Unknown

When I can't make a decision, it is because I am not present to my vision. It could be about getting up and running at 6:00 a.m. Do I stay in my warm bed or go outside in the cold morning air? When I can't choose, I look at my vision and weigh staying in bed against the healthy goals I have set for myself. My vision helps me make the decision.

• What is your vision for one area of your life?

• Why do you want to reinvent yourself?

• Are you stalled, bored, unclear or dissatisfied?

• Do you keep running into the same issues with decision-making, relationships or career progression?

Select an area of your life you would like to reinvent. What is it? Describe this area of your life as it is now, and how you would like it to be. Be specific and exact.

Commitment

Commitment is fundamental to a successful reinvention. It brings with it the power and freedom to create your life. First you have to get clear on what you want to reinvent. This could be reinventing your career, how you lead and communicate, how you make decisions, or how you relate to someone in your life.

Some people believe they lose freedom when they commit to someone or something. They feel as if they are closing off options. I ask you to contemplate the following possibility: *You gain freedom with commitment.* With commitment there is direction, power, clarity and enhanced decision-making.

When you clarify what you want to create and understand its value to you and others, you can commit to it and make better choices about how and where you spend your time. With intention, you can say yes to the things that are aligned with your commitments. You can make decisions and take actions that move you forward with your vision.

A client came to our coaching session frustrated and angry. She felt things were out of her control, and she was helpless to change anything. Her intention was to retire the following year from her executive position after being with the company for fifteen years. Throughout her employment, she had been compliant and easygoing, often working extraordinarily long hours with little social life. Since she was a widow, this had been easy to do because she could avoid focusing on any other part of her life outside of work. Eventually, this led to her decision to retire and reinvent her life.

Part of her reinvention was to allow herself to dream and imagine what a new life of adventure could look like. She committed to living a balanced life during the last year of her employment, began to focus on her well-being and explore what she wanted to do in retirement. One of her dreams was to live in Italy for three months after retiring. She committed to this and made plans to go to Italy to research how to make that happen. Then she was asked to participate in a company meeting that took place on the weekend she was supposed to fly to Milan!

I asked her to consider what she might be responsible for in this scenario. I wanted her to be accountable for her thoughts, feelings and interpretations. There is no right or wrong answer here. When you set out with an intention, you have choices and consequences for everything. When you choose to confront or avoid the consequences, you are either living or not living with intention.

My client realized she felt powerless and out of control, which caused her feelings of anger and resentment. She was forgetting she had choices.

She had been imagining scenarios that may or may not actually happen at work, such as being fired for not agreeing to attend the meeting. By not addressing the situation and appearing to be an easy-going, good employee, she felt victimized and at the mercy of her job. This was the moment of clarity for her; she had choices and was not powerless. She saw immediately what actions she could take.

The choices were uncomfortable, and she knew she needed to focus on her intention to live a balanced life and look at what was required to remain committed to that. Now, she could take action that was aligned with her reinvention. She could:

• Have a conversation with her bosses about the situation.

• Make a clear, powerful request to attend only a part of the meeting.

• Negotiate a situation where she could go to Milan *and* attend the meeting—an opportunity to have it all. This was her choice.

What was required in this situation? To reinvent the thinking that leads to feeling victimized, you must be willing to:

• Challenge automatic feelings of helplessness.

• Practice clear and powerful communication.

• Be creative and solution-oriented.

• Make bold requests and risk rejection.

• Be open to the possibility of creating a win for everyone.

Using these tools, my client attended the first day of the meeting and flew to Milan a day later. Instead of "playing nice," she was assertive, creative and bold—something she had not been for the past several years.

It is important to note that if she had avoided taking that action, she would still have chosen. If you choose to do nothing, you are making a choice.

When you are completely clear on what you are committed to, and you prioritize those commitments, you can choose powerfully. If I am not sure about something, all I have to do is check in with myself and see if the decision I need to make is aligned with my commitments. Interestingly, not having a commitment to something specific keeps me from making decisions! I use not making a commitment as a safety valve when I am afraid. Do you?

> *"There's a difference between interest and commitment. When you're interested in doing something, you do it only when circumstance permit. When you're committed to something, you accept no excuses, only results."*
> —Art Turock, American corporate leadership
> and motivational business speaker

If you are not committed one way or the other, how can you choose the best course of action? How will you choose where to place your priorities? Freedom comes in the ease of choosing an action aligned with your commitments.

Declaration

Are you the type of person who makes declarations all over the place but never follows through? Do you avoid making any declarations at all, so you cannot fail or disappoint people?

Declaration is an integral part of reinvention. Declaration is where the ideas become a formal statement of intention. For example, I was going through my own personal reinvention journey to transition from being a married business owner to being a single life and leadership coach. During my coach training program, I realized I needed to declare myself as a coach in order to begin building my practice as a professional coach, even though I did not have any clients as yet. This was difficult for me at first because I fretted people would view me as a fake, incompetent or unready. However, I realized I had to fully embrace my decision and vision to be a coach. I had to announce it to my network and own it, or I would be holding myself back. In the act of calling myself a coach and creating my business cards, I made a declaration that led me onto the path of having a successful professional coaching practice and one that is wholly sustained by referrals from friends and acquaintances.

Vision requires commitment, which leads to a declaration. Together, they move you forward to a successful reinvented life and career.

Reinvention with Intention Starts Now!

The moment I declared my reinvented intention as a life and leadership coach, I knew what was required to make it happen. I put a plan together and took actions that supported my vision.

My commitment guided me whenever I was hesitant. I am now activated by my motivation to lead by example and to live my purpose of inspiring others to live their lives with joyful intention.

All great leaders are visionaries who commit to and declare their commitment. Look at what you are wishing for and imagining. Notice what is missing or holding you back. Is your vision clear and compelling? Are you committed to it? How important is it for you to accomplish your vision? Have you made a formal declaration? Are you willing to be a great leader? Start now!

KAREN BÁEZ
Life & Leadership Coach

*Transforming thought presents
unlimited possibility*

(760) 594-1411

info@karenbaez.com

www.karenbaez.com

Karen Báez has always followed her dreams and is passionate about inspiring others to live theirs. She motivates leaders with compassion and creativity, supporting their transformation with unparalleled coaching tools and experience. She has held leadership roles in Europe, the Caribbean and New York City and was an award-winning sales manager for an international resort brand.

Relocating to San Diego, California, Karen established and sold a successful interior design business and co-founded a distribution company that developed a patented storage product. As vice president of operations and CFO, she guided sales to $4.2 million in five years.

Karen has coached and mentored other coaches to build their coaching practices and works with Vistage® International, the world's leading chief executive organization, to coach and support former CEOs to build and lead CEO peer groups to become better leaders, make better decisions and produce better results. She is the volunteer co-leader of the San Diego chapter of www.roomtoread.org, a nonprofit organization dedicated to providing education to children in developing countries and breaking the cycle of poverty through empowering a new generation of educated children.

Leadership Requires Vitality

By Carolyn Phillips, ACE

Are you experiencing the vitality and spring in your step that go with feelings of success, or do you feel burned out at the end of most days?

If you are not getting the most out of your day, if you are not concentrating and are running on empty, consider an overhaul of your business lifestyle. You can lead others only when you are full of energy yourself and can focus on results.

People easily fall into habits that lead to lackluster days and feelings of burnout. Some people are challenged because they sit at desks for eight hours. They need creative ways to get more movement during the day. Some people experience lack of energy because they skip meals. This promotes fat storage, weight gain and energy drain. Does any of this sound like you?

You can realize great results with planning and effort, including more vitality and good health. You spend time assessing a work project to find out what needs to be fixed or changed to get the best outcomes. This same planning works wonders for creating an abundance of vitality. You just need to identify problem areas and plan for your best health!

In more than twenty years of being a personal trainer and lifestyle and nutrition coach, I have worked with thousands of clients to inspire better health. Many factors greatly affect vitality—nutrition, exercise, lifestyle and stress are common contributors. It is important for you to understand the importance of each and how it influences your energy levels.

Here are some easy tips to incorporate into your business day. They can positively influence your lifestyle with true greatness and enhance your ability to lead your team to success!

"There is a vitality, a life force, an energy, a quickening, that is translated through you into action, and because there is only one of you in all time, this expression is unique."
—Martha Graham, American dancer, choreographer and teacher

Good Nutrition Creates Powerful Leaders

Nutrition is the cornerstone of good health; it is necessary to fight infections and disease and achieve vitality all day. It also is a key ingredient in having lots of energy and for optimizing brain chemistry and mental clarity. Knowing the value of good food is essential, so you can use it to positively affect your health and business vitality.

Eat and feel great. When you skip meals and snacks, you may think you are training your body to ignore hunger signals. However, when you do not eat regularly, your blood sugar level drops, and your energy levels pay the price. This habit needs to change in order to achieve a productivity boost at the office.

The solution is easy. Keep healthy, easy-to-eat snacks readily available in your desk. Almonds make a good snack when you feel a low energy slump. They lift your energy levels because they contain large amounts of iron and some B vitamins, which help your brain, nerves and muscles to function properly. Combine almonds with a source of vitamin C, such as an orange, so your body will better absorb the nutrients.

Remember vitamins and minerals. While food is the primary source of vitamins and minerals, food also releases carbohydrates, proteins and fats to give you energy, help fight infections and ward off disease. Support your food intake with a vitamin and mineral complex everyday. You will feel the difference from such a simple action.

Avoid additives. It is easy to snack from the vending machine at work or hit the fast food drive-through for a quick food fix. These choices typically serve up some of the unhealthiest nutrition options. Pack a lunch that includes organic foods and avoid processed foods, which have chemicals, decrease vitality and lead to overeating at the end of your day because they lack nutrients.

Become a "food detective" and carefully study food labels. Look for ingredients, additives and preservatives you need to avoid because they are energy zappers and are linked to obesity, health issues, mental deterioration and depression. Avoid sodium nitrite, enriched and bleached flour, saccharin, high fructose corn syrup, trans fats (partially hydrogenated oils), olestra, artificial coloring, high sodium content, monosodium glutamate (MSG) and sodium nitrate. These additives and preservatives are among the most questionable and are used primarily in foods with low nutritional value. It may be difficult to avoid these entirely. Read labels and try to limit them.

A good rule of thumb is this: If a food item has a long list of ingredients you cannot pronounce, there is probably more than one ingredient in it that could be harmful to your health. Generally, if a food contains more than ten ingredients, do not buy it.

Sugar zaps your immune system. Keeping a box of candy at your desk may seem like a sweet treat and warm welcome to coworkers, but sweets are short-term gratifications that come with a high price.

In addition to dulling your leadership edge, excess sugar consumption causes inflammation in your body, which leads to a sharp spike in insulin levels, and suppresses your immune system. When your immune system is suppressed, you get sick more often. Sugar accelerates the aging process and increases the risks of heart disease, every form of cancer, memory loss and energy drain.

I often hear people state they are "addicted to sugar." This is a true statement. Sugar causes your body to crave more sugar. According to the United States Department of Agriculture's Agriculture Fact Book 2001-2002, consumption of sugar since 1950 has increased 39 percent. The average person now consumes 52 added teaspoons of sugar daily!

When you read the ingredient contents of food, look at the grams of sugar listed on the label. If a nutrition label states a product has four grams of sugar, that means it contains one teaspoon of sugar. Also, beware of ingredients with the words "syrup," "sweetener" and anything ending in "-ose." These are all sugar!

If you choose to eat sugar, combine it with foods that have mono-unsaturated fats, such as nuts, olive oil and avocados. Fiber is also good since it aids in slowing down sugar absorption. You can find fiber in certain fruits, vegetables, whole grains, nuts and beans. Protein, too, aids in better sugar absorption, so include protein foods such as egg whites, chicken, fish, nuts and low fat dairy products.

Drink, drink, drink. If you need a quick energy boost, drink one or two glasses of water. Water is vital to proper body function and energy. Dehydration, even at minor levels, causes the body systems to slow down; this makes you feel sluggish, tired, irritable and less productive. Drinking water has other benefits, too, such as helping you avoid headaches and increase your metabolism.

Exercise and Good Lifestyle Choices Make Good Leaders

Mobility is essential for lasting eight hours—or more—at work, being pain free and remaining vital. A healthy lifestyle that includes exercise and movement positively affects body mass, increases heart and lung capacity, decreases depression and raises the overall quality of your life.

According to a 1996 report from the United States Attorney General, 25 percent of Americans are sedentary. In addition, a 2010 study by Ball State University's Center for Media Design found the typical person spends about forty hours per week in front of the TV and computer.

Many people think they have to feel motivated in order to exercise. Being inspired might help you get started, but motivation fades at some point. When motivation fades, remember the benefits of exercise—it can improve your mood and lift your spirits. Make sure you have a support system in place to encourage you. A certified and experienced personal trainer is an excellent person to help you develop strategies when your enthusiasm fades.

Weight training benefits. Weight training is the "miracle cure" for having great fitting clothing, an erect posture and for stress relief. Why weight training?

According to experts at the President's Council for Fitness, Sport & Nutrition, www.fitness.gov, as you age, your muscles atrophy, and you lose approximately five pounds of muscle tissue every ten years due to factors such as poor nutrition and lack of a resistance program. Losing five pounds of muscle means you are burning 300 calories less each day.

The next time you hear someone say, "My metabolism is slowing down as I get older," you will know one of the reasons why. If you start or maintain a weight-training program along with better nutrition, you can add about five pounds of muscle tissue in approximately three months to a year, depending on genetics and other factors. Your metabolism will increase as your lean mass increases from a good weight-training program.

Cindy is a business owner who came to work with me because she did not know how to begin putting together a plan to get in better shape. She stated "lack of time" was her biggest obstacle, along with not knowing what to do first. She believed being in better shape would make her feel better when she spoke in front of large groups. She also wanted to set a better example for her team at work, and she, of course, wanted to feel more energetic all day long.

Our first step as we started working together was to find ways to increase movement during her day that were easy to incorporate into her lifestyle. Cindy started taking the stairs and walking more, and she stopped parking in the spot closest to the front door. Instead of emailing a coworker, she would get up and walk over to the person. She also started sitting on a stability ball—a soft, elastic exercise ball filled with air—to engage and strengthen her core.

Family life after work mostly consisted of food and television in the evening or finishing work started earlier in the day. One night, Cindy was in her home office finishing up for the evening, when she heard her husband in the kitchen, and she called out, "Eric, can you bring me a glass of water?" Then she had an "a-ha" moment and realized how she was consistently finding ways to move *less* in her day. Maybe it was not just "lack of time" that was creating her problem.

I suggested she arise fifteen minutes earlier every day and add some form of weight training in her home office area. At the end of one month, we evaluated her energy levels, posture and overall emotions. We also looked at her newly-toned muscles and how her clothing fit. Setting short-term goals, seeing great results and feeling better gave Cindy the jump-start she needed to begin living a more active lifestyle.

Cardiovascular benefits. A brisk thirty-minute walk can help calm you down while providing a quick pick-me-up. Cardiovascular exercise delivers oxygen and nutrients to your tissues. When your heart and lungs work more efficiently, you have more energy to complete your workday with ease. It is also a great time to reflect and plan your day.

"All parts of the body which have a function if used in moderation and exercised in labors in which each is accustomed, become thereby healthy, well developed and age more slowly, but if unused they become liable to disease, defective in growth and age quickly."
—Hippocrates, ancient Greek physician

Looking for a timesaving workout? Try circuit training, which combines strength training with cardiovascular activities, and provides a more time-efficient workout than traditional aerobic and weight training sessions. In just thirty minutes, you can improve your mood, feel happier, become more relaxed while boosting your self-confidence and self-esteem.

Stress busting benefits. Reducing stress—external or internal—will reduce free radical damage, slow down the aging process and increase your energy and mental capacity. If you want your body to look and feel better, have more energy, develop a stronger immune system and have clear and vibrant skin, it is essential to work on ways to reduce your stress. Here are some basics to consider:

- **Caffeine.** A favorite pick-me-up is coffee. While it may give you a short-lived boost, it has a downside. Too much insulin has an adverse effect on the immune system, brain cells and sugar metabolism. Caffeine acts as a diuretic, depleting the body of fluids and minerals, particularly calcium and zinc. In addition, it can stimulate elevations in heart rate and blood pressure. Try substituting a decaf green or white tea or try a naturally decaffeinated red tea for all the benefits of the antioxidants found in them.

- **Sleep.** The quantity and quality of sleep are both important. The Health Promotion Center of Dartmouth College (www.dartmouth.edu/~healthed) recommends between seven and eight hours of sleep a night for adults. To get a good night's sleep, avoid stimulants in the evening, including caffeine, sodas or chocolate. Alcohol may help you get to sleep, but it will cause you to wake up throughout the night. Try chamomile tea, which is known for being a good sleep aid. To improve sleep, do something for yourself every day to reduce stress and include some type of exercise early in the day.

- **Posture.** Good posture opens the chest cavity and increases oxygen intake. One of the biggest culprits for bad posture is sitting at your desk all day without taking a break. The body was not designed to be in a seated position for long periods. Sitting in a chair promotes weak abdominal muscles and contributes to weak back muscles. Blood also pools in your legs, which reduces blood flow to the brain and other important muscles.

- **Breaks.** Take a break once an hour. Take a mini-breathing break (see below), climb a stairway or stretch. You can do office stretches while seated at your desk, standing in your workspace or on a conference call.

- **Breathe.** Build in mini-breathing breaks during your day. Take three deep breaths and release them slowly to relieve stress. Oxygen increases the energy available for your brain and muscles. This kind of quick break only takes moments, and you may feel like your stress is floating away, giving you a chance to calm down and focus better on the task at hand.

Take Action and Use Your Body to Be a Better Leader

Vitality is a major factor in being a strong leader. Taking care of your body, mind and spirit is an inside job that only you can do.

• What areas of your life can you change? Focus on improving nutrition, increasing exercise or decreasing stress and plan to replace any habits that drain your zest for life.

• Get help planning your schedule or doing chores. Use the time you save to recharge and energize yourself.

• Treat yourself to massages, a relaxing bath or a fitness class with good friends to give your body and mind the pick-me-up they need.

• Treat yourself to a "time-for-you" activity at least once a week. Think of this as the "edge to recharge" so you can be a more productive, savvy leader.

By implementing even some of these tips into your lifestyle, you may find that you are easily reclaiming the vitality you need as a leader. You can then lead others to their new vital lifestyles.

CAROLYN PHILLIPS, ACE

Founder, Fit Behavior

(860) 529-9867

www.fitbehavior.com

carolyn@fitbehavior.com

Carolyn Phillips has been an ACE certified personal trainer, lifestyle and weight management professional for more than twenty years. She is passionate about motivating, educating and supporting individuals in living healthier lives. Carolyn teaches health and vitality and inspires people to choose healthy habits and live them every day.

Carolyn graduated from Quinnipiac University with a bachelor of arts degree in organizational leadership. In 1997, she founded Fit Behavior, which offers group fitness classes, group and one-on-one personal training and massage therapy. A state- and national-level champion in bodybuilding, mountain biking, volleyball and gymnastics, Carolyn has won the Forty under 40 Award® for outstanding leadership for the Greater Hartford, Connecticut area. She has been featured on television and radio, is a regular speaker at corporations and women's events and writes for several lifestyle publications.

Carolyn is president of the board for Chrysalis Center, Inc.,® a private, nonprofit healthcare agency, which provides rehabilitation and health care support to individuals and families.

Using Intuition and Insight to Become a Better Leader

By Marci Nemhauser, PsyD, PCC

For many years, I listened to women talk about "getting a gut feeling" or "acting on a hunch" and I did not hear men speaking like this. I realized I regularly tuned into my intuition to check out a perception. I have found it to be an important part of my leadership toolbox, and I began to explore the difference between men and women in this regard.

Many books are being written about new findings in brain research and the fields of neurobiology and neuropsychiatry. They all speak to this fact: There are biological differences in how female and male brains function. I believe these findings will change how you view yourself as a leader.

Michael Ugrian with Barbara Annis wrote a groundbreaking book entitled Leadership and the Sexes, published by Jossey-Bass in 2008. It focuses on how women and men lead differently and cites new brain science to support their conclusions. These differences do not make one gender superior to the other. Rather, when you understand the differences and work with them, you become a more effective leader. You can make a significant impact in your work, your family and your life by understanding how women are wired for leadership. This understanding will enhance your ability to succeed.

"Common sense tells us that males and females behave differently. Girls arrive already wired as girls, and boys arrive already biologically wired as boys. Their brains are different by the time they are born, and their brains are what drive their impulses, values and their very realities."
—LuAnn Brizendine, MD, American author and neuropsychiatrist

Using Your Women's Intuition

Among many old wives' tales, an enduring one is that women have a "sixth sense" or intuition. This is the ability to take in information through the senses, in addition to rational data, and to understand this information on a deeper level.

Have you ever experienced a feeling of discomfort when nothing tangible has occurred to cause this sensation? For example, in a meeting with coworkers, have you suddenly gotten a sense of tension between two people even though they were not acting any differently? Did you later discover one of them was angry with the other? Your intuition noticed something was going on under the surface.

Women pick up and absorb information in a variety of ways. We tend to use all of our senses to scan the environment and "take the temperature" of a room. This may originate from our early cave-dweller days when women tended the cave and the children while the men went hunting. It was imperative for the survival of the group that women be alert to potential dangers to protect the clan.

You can use your body language to communicate what you are not verbalizing. Your facial expressions speak more loudly than your voice. You are constantly receiving cues and clues as you interact with others. However, many people rarely use the information they receive this way.

Understanding and using the clues you receive about other people's body language can give you a sense about what is happening in the room. Generally, women tend to be more observant of the people and things in their environment than men are.

Allan and Barbara Pease, authors of *The Definitive Book of Body Language,* published by Bantam in 2006, studied how people understand and process body language. They set up a mirror in a hotel lobby and covered part of it with plants, so the face of the person looking in the mirror could not be seen. Several different people walked into the hotel lobby, saw the image and went over to the registration desk. When asked if they had recognized the other guest, 85 percent of men answered no. Most men failed to recognize themselves in the mirror. On the other hand, 58 percent of the women knew it was a mirror and thirty percent said the other guest looked familiar.

Today, as a woman leader, you can use these same tools to help you more effectively present to your team or group. Let's say you are presenting the new direction you want your department to take, and you notice several people using their cell phones or computers. Others appear disengaged. You have the opportunity to address these responses in the moment and have a more authentic dialogue with your team.

You can use many sources to make sense of interpersonal interactions. If you choose to use and understand those sources, you can gain a distinct advantage over those who remain unconscious to this wonderful tool!

"Nothing in life is to be feared. It is only to be understood."
—Marie Curie, Polish-born French physicist and Nobel Prize winner

"TA DA!"

This acronym stands for: Take, Assess, Discern, Act.

In graduate school, I created acronyms to help me remember diagnostic categories. During exams, I found I could recall the acronym and then recall the information. As I started thinking about ways to support people as they stepped into leadership roles, I identified key things that would help empower them. Because I believe we remember something that has a little humor involved, I created the acronym *TA DA*.

Take in information using all your senses. Notice where people choose to sit, who takes lots of space at the table and who takes up less space. Pay attention to the sounds and tone of someone's voice and how he or she expresses opinions. People tend to sit where they feel comfortable, safe and powerful. Observe who sits next to whom. These become working hypotheses about what might be the unspoken conversations going on during the meeting. You take in information constantly—pay attention to it.

Assess what this information means. You can sense when someone is not saying exactly what he or she really feels or means. You notice strain or tension in the person's voice. Pay attention to these clues! They tell you how to ask follow-up questions that move the conversation along and uncover the real issues.

Discern and decide what and how much of this information you will use. There might be a conversation behind the conversation— something is not being said. How might this help you better understand group dynamics? Notice people's body language while you listen to them. Pay attention to reactions.

Act on what you have determined to be an appropriate response to the information you have received. Tune in to your inner self and notice what you feel is your next move. Decide how to create a meaningful message from your observations. Making an observation about something you have seen inspires others to feel and act more openly about reporting what they also are observing.

I remember a time when I walked into a room to give a presentation to the executive team of a small company. As I entered, I sensed something unsettling. My heart started racing, and my stomach clenched. Now, this is not unusual for me when I am about to present, although this time I noticed I felt differently. I walked in, put my materials on the table and then took a deep breath. As I did this, I also "tuned in" to the sensations I was experiencing in my body. My eyes felt teary and my chest felt tight.

I stood in front of the group and asked this question, "Did something out of the ordinary happen today?"

After a moment of silence, the CEO responded. One of the members of the executive team had been killed in a car accident the night before. Needless to say, the work I did with the team that day was very different from what I had planned to do.

If I had ignored my instinct and proceeded with my own agenda, the group would not have been able to focus, and I would have been less successful. Instead, we spent the time discussing loss and change and the impact the death of this person had on everyone.

You have these same resources readily available all the time. Knowing how to use them makes you better at what you do. There is a method I have developed that makes this easy to learn.

Gutsy Leadership

Being a gutsy leader is a three-part process that gives you the potential to reach people on many different levels and be more successful as a leader. It means you need guts to lead! Here is how to put this method into action:

Paint the picture. When it is time for you to present your vision or ideas to your team, know that people hear in different ways. You will be more effective with your audience if you use words that connect with all styles.

- **Visual listeners.** There are people who hear what you say by creating pictures in their minds. It is important to include descriptions and images in your conversations to help visual listeners "see" what you are saying. For example, to capture the attention of the visual listener, use descriptive words or diagrams to explain what you want. Visual listeners also like colors and respond to visual terms, such as "Let's look at this," "Show me what you mean," and "This appears right."

- **Auditory listeners.** For listeners who are auditory in their style, make sure to include words that create sounds. This could be something as simple as making sure you use phrases such as, "This will create a big splash in the market" or "This sounds like a good idea." In addition, you probably want to change the inflection of your voice to create vocal interest and meaning.

- **Kinesthetic listeners** need words that convey action. Phrases such as "Let's move forward," or "We have to seize the moment" impact people who "hear" through movement. For those who are kinesthetic listeners, use words that describe action and where your plan will move the group.

As a leader, you have a responsibility to make your ideas and vision understood. You want others to support you. Including words that appeal to all types of listeners will invite people to join you in your mission. They will feel included in the plan and make it their own. This helps you move successfully in the direction you want to go.

> *"A leader takes people where they want to go. A great leader takes people where they don't necessarily want to go but ought to be."*
> —Rosalynn Carter, former first lady of the United States

Be a change agent. You, as the leader, hold the vision to move the organization forward. Therefore, you need to be clear about what you want and where you want to go. You are the catalyst for the change and the source of the outcome you desire.

Not all people view change as an exciting prospect. Some love the familiar and crave the routine. These people may view change as threatening and work to keep things the same. Have you ever experienced a time when you introduced a new concept or innovation you wanted to implement, and several people came up with all the ways it just would not work? If you are a mother, you have probably experienced this even when you just wanted to change the bedtime schedule!

The unknown can be scary. Stepping into a new area where the rules are unfamiliar and the goals are different can be a daunting task. Invite others to share their concerns and encourage collaborative solutions.

For those who view change as exciting and refreshing, your role is to make sure you capture and maintain everyone's enthusiasm and steer it in the direction you want to go. When a change is about to occur, people may look for ways to slow things down. They will say the subject needs more study, or you need to gather more input from others. This is a way to derail the project in hopes the change does not need to occur. Listen to the objections, acknowledge people's input and do not get distracted.

Lead from behind. My mentor, Dr. Bill Korach, speaks of leadership as creating the conditions for other people's success. Over the years, I have come to understand this to be a powerful and effective way to be a gutsy leader. In 1988, I was the chair of a campaign for my school district. I had a core group of dedicated, creative and passionate people. This was the first time this group had come together to work on a single project. I realized each person had unique skills, and my job was to become the catalyst for unleashing their power and making sure each had what they needed to be successful—which they did, and the project succeeded.

In a company—or even in a family—success comes by communicating, collaborating and sharing a vision. As an effective leader, you want others to want to join you in this shared idea. Every person has individual talents. Truly transformational change happens when individuals collaborate and create something that is far greater than the sum of the individual contributions.

Sharing the glory and the spotlight with all of the contributors creates a lasting bond and connection. It generates empowerment and encourages others to step into new roles and to grow. Leaders who always need to have center stage will de-motivate employees. On the other hand, celebrating others' successes builds the belief that everyone is important and everyone makes a difference. This generates loyalty and creativity. For more on this subject, see "Playing Win-Win" by Elizabeth Agnew on page 113.

What Is Next?

You have discovered a connection between your inner and outer self. Use this connection as a powerful tool as you develop your leadership skills. By tuning in to your inner guidance system, you use all your senses and intuitive abilities to keep you informed of what is happening beneath the surface.

"There is something in every one of you that waits and listens for the sound of the genuine in yourself. It is the only true guide you will ever have. And if you cannot hear it, you will all of your life spend your days on the ends of strings that somebody else pulls."
—Howard Thurman, American theologian and activist

By heightening your awareness and sharpening your listening skills, you will become a truly amazing leader! These skills take practice. Here are some quick pointers to keep in mind:

• Make sure you enter a conversation with your senses alert to the nuances behind the spoken words.

• Allow yourself to feel what conversation might be taking place beneath the one that you are engaged in at the moment.

• Watch for clues from other people in their body language and how they express their ideas.

• Be more interested in what the person is saying rather than on what you are planning to say in response.

• Ask clarifying questions more than cross-examining ones.

• Look people in the eye when you are talking with them.

• Smile when it is appropriate, and let people finish their sentences.

You can be a powerful leader by being in touch with your intuition— this ability sets you apart from others. Practice tuning in to yourself to take your leadership skills to an entirely new level.

MARCI NEMHAUSER, PsyD, PCC
Professional Growth Services

Ignite Your Life!

(503) 684-5322

marci@professionalgrowthservices.com

www.professionalgrowthservices.com

Since 1987, clinical psychologist and executive and personal coach Marci Nemhauser, PsyD, PCC, has shown hundreds of people how to handle issues of depression, anxiety and post-traumatic stress. She works with people facing increased demands on their time and helps them find balance and meaning, confront and manage the challenges they face every day and co-create tools that enable them to thrive.

Marci is active in her community and has served on her local school board for many years. She co-teaches leadership at the Lake Oswego Chamber of Commerce and serves on the board of the Women's Center for Leadership.® She gives keynote addresses and leads workshops on the "Unique Style of Women's Leadership" and "Women, Power and Politics." She is passionate about public education and believes all children need an excellent education in order to be active citizens. She works with high school students and their parents to improve communication and relationship skills.

Married since 1969, Marci has two married children and two grandsons. Becoming a grandmother was her most life-transforming event! Her grandsons inspire her to be in the moment and see life as a constant place of discovery.

Success Appeal
Show Up as the Leader You Are
By Karen Solomon

Each of us forms perceptions and interpretations based on the lenses and filters of our unique life experiences. From the perspective of my role as an image consultant, life coach and Speaking Circles® facilitator, I teach women and men how to show up in the world in a way that is consistent with their level of leadership and their expertise.

It is not enough to simply earn the academic or work experience required to be an expert or leader in your field. You must physically present yourself like a leader as well. In other words, you must look the part of your role in the world if you want to be taken seriously. I am talking about your clothing, your level of confidence and your personal magnetism or charisma.

If your client or audience is distracted by any aspect of how you look, speak or act, your ability to be perceived as the savvy leader you are can be sabotaged—no matter how qualified you are or how valuable your information is. Your clothing, posture, body language, hairstyle, smile, and how you relate to others are all means of communication. Consider these factors to be equally as important, if not more so, than what you have to say.

How you present yourself makes a statement about who you are. When you are in a position of leadership and are more visible in the world, your choices are critical. You have worked hard at attaining the mastery and expertise that qualifies you for your leadership position. Now take yourself to another level of leadership by mastering the following three C's:

• Clothing and style

• Confidence

• Charisma

Clothing and Style

The clothing you wear can help bring out your power, or it can undermine your success. People form immediate opinions and judgments, both positive and negative, upon first seeing you. Since you do not get a second chance to make a great first impression, you must do it right the first time.

As Anne Hollander wrote in her book *Seeing Through Clothes,* published by Viking Press in 1978, "Despite all ideological attempts to transcend the mode in clothes, it is the lust of the eye for change, the power of the eye to make instant associations, and its need to demand and to create and combine images that hold clothing to significant and delicate shifts of dynamic visual form."

Deliberate, discerning style choices can enhance your ability to look like the leader you are and can give you the confidence required to earn the respect of others.

One of the most important considerations for you or any leader is to dress appropriately for the venue and demographic of the people to whom you will be presenting. The First Lady of the United States, Michele Obama, is a good example. She wears haute couture dresses while hosting White House affairs. However, when she meets with schoolchildren, she wears casual clothing from more affordable stores such as the Gap.® I recommend that you do advance research to determine the age and generation of your client or audience. It is no fun to find yourself feeling out of place because you are either overdressed or underdressed for a venue or occasion. Do your homework.

Janice, a client of mine, interviewed for a top-level executive position with a company specializing in high-end athletic gear. The company is managed and staffed by young, hip people in their 20s and 30s, spanning Generations X and Y. Janice is approaching 50, and she had a conservative wardrobe. Together, we developed a more contemporary, fashion-forward style, and Janice felt comfortable and confident in her new look. The company was equally impressed.

Linda, a skilled executive coach and consultant with an MBA, was in her mid-thirties when she came to me for assistance with her image. A lovely, petite, blonde-haired woman with an hourglass figure, she found herself not being taken seriously by her clients who were at least a decade older than she was. It was necessary for her to present herself in a more mature and professional manner. Our goal was to give her a more tailored wardrobe that would elicit the respect required for her professional credibility. Given her proportions, and the fact that the human eye tends to be drawn to imbalances, we played down her shapely body and chose accessories that were understated and classic. Her transformation and new look increased the level of confidence she needed to attract the business she wanted, and she was well on her way to filling her consulting practice.

Both Linda and Janice's stories exemplify how changing your wardrobe can have a positive effect on your self-confidence and on how others perceive you. Here are some image tips for you to consider as a savvy leader:

- Dress according to your venue and target audience.

- Your clothing should showcase you, not scream for attention. Think of yourself as the artwork and your clothing as the frame.

- The human eye is drawn toward imbalances. Dress to downplay any physical attribute that calls too much attention to itself.

- Wear your best colors to command attention, gain credibility and enhance your self-confidence. If you do not know which colors are best for you, consider hiring a color expert or an image consultant.

- Be prepared! Plan what you will wear in advance of any important meetings or dates. Last minute surprises, such as a stain or rip, can be stressful.

- Footwear can make or break an outfit. Keep your shoes shined, well maintained and in style.

- Update your hairstyle—keep your cut and color current.

- Your accessories should complement your outfit, not overpower it.

- A great handbag or briefcase can complete your ensemble to perfection.

My client Barbara is a top software designer in the entertainment business. She went to Tokyo to present a new product to a number of prospective buyers. Upon her return, she recounted what it was like to wait for her highly anticipated appointment with the head of Sony Entertainment.®

Barbara recounted, "The walls were covered in autographed photos and movie memorabilia. For a moment, I panicked. What was I doing here? Then, I looked down at my oh-so-stylish shoes and sleek, black leather portfolio and realized that even though I was nervous, I looked the part of the successful and creative software designer I am!" Her confidence was renewed, and she completed her meeting with a new contract for her products.

Confidence

Confidence is the belief in yourself and your abilities. How you feel about yourself affects the way you act, and the way you act is a major factor in how other people perceive you. Most successful leaders typically radiate self-confidence. They display certitude and assurance and evoke others' trust in them. They respect themselves and thus earn the respect of others because they emanate security and a sense of self-worth. They command attention and attract success. Your self-confidence is crucial if you want to be respected as a leader.

> *"A good leader inspires people to have confidence in the leader, a great leader inspires people to have confidence in themselves."*
> —Eleanor Roosevelt, American, former first lady of the United States

You can change your life and your outlook by developing your confidence. When Sharon began her coaching relationship with me, she had just earned a master of business administration degree from Stanford University and was working in a leadership position in the field of human resources at a financial institution, However, Sharon did not feel like the successful young woman she was. We worked on improving her level of confidence by putting the above tips, among others, into action.

After months of working with me, Sharon wrote the following, "I'm still pinching myself at how radically different my life is today than it was a year ago. The serious investment I have made in myself has paid off! Through eating a healthier diet and working out regularly, I have lost weight. In addition to being thinner and looking better, I have never felt stronger, more present or more powerful. I have entered into two of the best relationships I have ever had. The first is with myself, and the second is with a wonderful, spirited, life-loving man who has exceeded my expectations for how love can feel. We're moving in together next month."

Here are some qualities confident people have in common that you can cultivate for yourself:

• Confident people make good eye contact.

• They are prepared and put together in all ways.

• People with confidence radiate health and vitality. Most confident leaders are physically fit and feel good about their bodies. For more on this subject, see "Leadership Requires Vitality" by Carolyn Phillips on page 67.

• They have a sense of humor and smile a lot.

• Self-confident people have good posture.

• They take responsibility for themselves in all aspects of their lives, both professional and personal.

• Confident people do not become defensive when receiving criticism. They listen to feedback and use it to evaluate their performance.

Charisma

As important as it is to dress appropriately and have self-confidence, it is the charisma or magnetism, charm and presence you emanate, that will establish you as a leader with true success appeal.

> *"Charisma is a sparkle in people that money can't buy. It's an invisible energy with visible effects."*
> —Marianne Williamson, American author, lecturer and activist

A charismatic leader has a natural ability to captivate and influence others. She radiates extraordinary power and inspires people with her appealing personality. When I think of charismatic people, I see individuals who are authentic with a remarkable ability to connect deeply with others.

Lynne Twist, co-founder of The Pachamama Alliance and author of *The Soul of Money,* published by W. W. Norton & Company in 2006, is one of the most charismatic women I know. Her enthusiasm for the many projects with which she is involved is contagious. When Lynne connects with you for even a moment, she makes you feel as though you are the only person in the room, even if she is addressing a crowd of thousands. In addition, Lynne's warmth, authenticity, compassion and ability to freely share her emotions serve her well in her capacity as an internationally known fundraiser, speaker and author.

Bill Clinton, former president of the United States, combines his tremendous intellectual capacity with his enormous heart. He holds court everywhere he goes and seems to enjoy every person he meets. He listens, understands and displays what looks like sincere and innate affection for people who are going through difficult times. President Clinton's eight years in office as well as his extraordinary humanitarian work exemplify his style of charismatic leadership.

In Michael Ellsberg's book, *The Power of Eye Contact: Your Secret for Success in Business, Love, and Life,* published by HarperCollins in 2010, the author writes that people who experience Bill Clinton in person usually report that they feel like they are the only people in the room. According to Ellsberg, this is the transcendent power of eye contact. It is " . . . the ability to forge a connection so strong between humans, in so short a time, that two people feel like one in an instant. I know of no other force in human experience that can work such magic so quickly."

You might not be as naturally charismatic as Lynne Twist or President Clinton. However, you can certainly cultivate behaviors and actions that will empower your authentic leadership style.

Through my willingness to simply be with people through eye contact, I have had some of the most intimate and lovely experiences with children and adults during my international travels, particularly throughout Southeast Asia and Latin America. Unlike the United States, these are cultures where children openly and unabashedly stare at people, fascinated by our differences. I love to gaze back at them. It is an enriching experience to connect with people in this way—two people simply being present and experiencing connection without saying a word. Lee Glickstein, the creator of Speaking Circles, has named this phenomenon, "Relational Presence."

I have witnessed the power of eye contact and relational presence repeatedly during my years as a Speaking Circles facilitator. In a matter of just a few minutes of standing in front of an audience, people run the gamut of emotions from shyness to fear to love as they allow themselves to simply see and be seen. A small, yet profound, action can generate huge results. If you are not accustomed to being with people in this way, I suggest you start making eye contact with your clients, friends and family members until it becomes second nature.

Here are some specific tips to keep in mind when you start any presentation:

Make and maintain good eye contact. When speaking either to an individual or in front of an audience, take a deep breath, become aware of your feet on the ground and make eye contact with first one, then another two or three people without saying a word. The few seconds you commit to being quiet, rather than launching right into your presentation, will create a safe space for your audience. You will meet them in the silence. For more about the power of this kind of practice, see the chapter "Maximizing Your Everyday Moments of Truth" by Ann Kelley on page 123.

Communicate like a leader. Charismatic leaders naturally know how to relate to people and draw them in.

- Emulate these leaders by personalizing your presentations with stories and examples to which your audience can relate. This creates camaraderie and makes your message memorable.

- Address people by name to capture their attention and show your interest in them. The act of saying their name will help you remember it.

- Give heartfelt compliments that give people a boost and help them feel good about themselves and you.

- Smile. A simple smile is one of the best and quickest ways of making yourself instantly more likeable and approachable.

Oprah Winfrey is an excellent example of a leader who communicates using all of the above.

Show Up as the Leader You Are

Some confident, charismatic people were born with these characteristics. Others have learned how to develop them through practice and by working with coaches, consultants and mentors. Apply these techniques immediately to enhance the influence you already have in your leadership position. Here is a quick summary:

Your clothing and style. Take an honest inventory of your physical appearance. When you intend to show up as a leader, be sure your style is congruent with your brand, and your clothing reflects your leadership role.

Your confidence. Project a level of confidence pertinent to the savvy leader you are by being prepared and put together.

Your charisma. Powerful leaders differentiate themselves by connecting with people through eye contact, heartfelt compliments and genuine enthusiasm.

Immediately apply these compelling action steps and you will be taken seriously as the leader you are. Your ability to relate to people authentically and personally will be enhanced. To improve your eye contact and communication skills, consider participating in a Speaking Circle. More information about Speaking Circles can be found at www.speakingcircles.com. Polish your image and presentation by hiring an expert image consultant or coach.

Accelerate your success appeal starting now. Which of the three C's—clothing, confidence and charisma—needs your attention? Take action to show up as the leader you are!

KAREN SOLOMON
Success Appeal™

Complete Confidence from the
Bedroom to the Boardroom™

(707) 540-5909

karen@successappeal.com

www.successappeal.com

Karen Solomon inspires her clients to recognize, own and convey charisma. She integrates a solid foundation as an academically-trained educator with 25 years of experience as an image consultant, Speaking Circles® facilitator and coach. Karen develops and leads seminars and delivers keynote speeches. She shows clients and audiences how to physically present themselves to the outside world congruent with who they are on the inside.

In her popular program, *Men, Sex & Money*,® Karen teaches women communication skillsets for healthy sustainable relationships. Whether helping you dress for an important job interview, assisting you in cultivating a whole new style or suggesting ways to improve your relationship, Karen's sense of humor adds fun to any situation.

A breast cancer survivor herself, Karen advocates for women undergoing life-threatening illnesses. Karen is a stewardship circle member of the Pachamama Alliance and facilitates the Awakening the Dreamer Symposium. When she is not mentoring young women, volunteering for hospice, skiing, practicing Spanish or traveling, Karen enjoys the company of friends and family. She lives in the San Francisco Bay Area.

The Savvy Woman's Guide to a Polished Image

By Laura Rubeli

Your professional image says a lot about who you are inside. Within seconds of meeting someone, they can assess your education level, financial stability and confidence—all based on your appearance.

Success depends on how you are perceived by others. To get promotions and pay increases, you need to look the part as well as deliver outstanding work results. When you are well-dressed, others may automatically assume you are educated, financially stable, capable and confident. Your professional appearance may be the one factor that sets you apart from colleagues with the same expertise and education. Dressing to influence may give you the edge you need to secure the next well-deserved promotion or client.

I became aware of professional dress when I started working on Wall Street in New York City. I was 22 years old and had no idea what business dress was. I wanted to climb the corporate ladder and soon realized that when I dressed the part of an executive, I instantly felt capable and confident. Dressing like an executive gave me the confidence necessary to succeed.

Harvard Business Review published a blog on February 9, 2011 written by Sylvia Ann Hewlett called "Dressing for the job you want?"

Hewlett states: "Women, in particular, believed that dressing the part was a vital factor in attaining success: 53% of them felt aspiring female execs needed to toe a very conservative line, avoiding flashy make-up, plunging necklines, too-short or too-tight skirts, and long fingernails." Hewlett goes on to write, "Half the women surveyed and 37% of the men considered appearance and executive presence to be intrinsically linked—they understood that if you don't look the part of a leader, you're not likely to be given the role."

> *"What a strange power there is in clothing."*
> —Isaac Bashevis Singer, Jewish-American

Dress codes are an integral part of the workplace in any organization. Whether your company's environment is creative or has a very traditional business culture, employees may be expected to follow certain guidelines regarding their dress. If your organization does not have a written dress code, the following style scale is a great guideline to help get you started.

Judith Rasband, founder and director of the Conselle Insititute of Image Management, developed the following Style Scale that shows the four levels of professional dress.

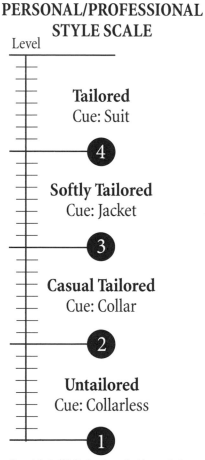

PERSONAL/PROFESSIONAL STYLE SCALE

Level

Tailored
Cue: Suit

4

Softly Tailored
Cue: Jacket

3

Casual Tailored
Cue: Collar

2

Untailored
Cue: Collarless

1

Copyright Judith Rasband, used with permission

Here is how the Style Scale works, from the most formal to the least formal.

Tailored Level 4

This style of dress communicates _authority, credibility, capability_ and _responsibility._

This level is the most authoritative of business clothing. It is appropriate for executive roles and businesses, such as banking, accounting and law and also for an interview in those fields or interaction with an important client for the first time.

Typical situations to wear tailored dress include:

• Leading a formal meeting or conference

• Making a formal presentation

• Formal cocktail networking

• Representing your company in public

Key elements in this level of dress are a matched suit and hosiery. The tailored level of dress for women includes a:

• Matched suit skirt, suit jacket, or pantsuit with a shirt or blouse

• Matched dress and jacket

• Coatdress

• Matched pantsuit-slacks and a jacket with a shirt or blouse

Clothing at this level of dress are designed with predominately straight lines, angular shapes, and dark colors. The clothes are structured and include a collar and lapel.

Softly Tailored Level 3

This style of dress communicates the traits *accessibility, receptiveness,* and *trust.*

This level includes business casual looks. It is appropriate for sales and service jobs and creative businesses, such as advertising, architecture, interior design, education and fashion. The softly tailored level aids in creating an informal, yet orderly work environment. It will position you as a leader who is knowledgeable in their field.

Typical situations to wear softly tailored dress include:

• Leading less formal to informal meetings or conferences

• Making a less formal presentation

• Informal networking

• Less formal meetings with clients or customers who wear relatively more casual clothes

Key elements in this level of dress is a jacket or blazer. The softly tailored level of dress for women includes:

• An unmatched skirt or pants and jacket with a shirt or blouse

• A dress with a jacket or blazer

• A shirtwaist dress

The clothing in this level of dress is designed with some softer curved lines and design elements such as lighter jacket colors. It's the mix or combination of design elements from tailored and untailored looks that creates the message appropriate for this business casual look.

Casual Tailored Level 2

This style of dress communicates the traits *approachable, knowledgeable, cooperative* and *conscientious.*

This level of style also includes business casual looks appropriate for people oriented businesses. It is appropriate for professionals in computer programming, education, medicine and social work.

Typical situations to wear casual tailored dress include:

• Making a casual, preliminary presentation

• Relaxed office meetings

• Casual visits with customers known to wear very casual clothes

• Casual networking

Key element is a collar. Casual tailored dress for women includes:

• A skirt or pants and shirt with a collar

• A skirt or pants and shirt with a collar, with a sweater or vest

• Knit dresses, float dresses, jumpers

Casual tailored clothes are mixed with untailored design elements such as softer, more pliable fabrics in a greater variety of colors.

Untailored Level 1

This casual look communicates the traits *informal, hard-working, dependable,* and *relaxed.*

This level is for very relaxed professions, such as sports professionals, fast food uniforms, construction workers, maintenance and landscape artists that require flexible but durable clothing.

Key element is a top with no collar. Untailored dress for women includes:

- Jeans, shorts, sweatpants

- T-shirts, tank tops

- Sundresses

Untailored clothes have relaxed shapes, curved lines and lighter colors.

Always remember—assumptions may be made on your intelligence and capabilities based on your appearance. When dressing for work, always answer these questions:

- What message am I communicating?

- What is the image I want to portray?

- Am I going to be taken seriously?

- Am I approachable?

- Do I look authoritative?

Here are a few general guidelines on how to dress to influence in the workplace.

- Your clothing should fit well and be neatly pressed.

- Always choose a professional wardrobe that you like. Your goal is to receive positive feedback from people who are knowledgeable about your industry standard of clothing.

- Keep your look simple and successful until you become accustomed to the environment and your company's dress code.

- For traditional businesses, wear hosiery in a neutral color. For creative industries that require a softly tailored level of dress, you may wear hosiery that coordinates with your skirt or dress.

- Do not carry a purse with a briefcase. Choose one or the other.

- Always make sure your shoes are clean and polished.

- Be sure your shirts and dresses are not too low-cut. A provocative outfit can jeopardize your professional image.

- Tattoos should be covered to avoid distraction.

Dressing for Your Body Type

"Fashion is architecture, it is a matter of proportions."
—Coco Chanel, French fashion designer

Dressing well is about wearing clothes that fit and flatter your individual body type. Everyone is unique. Knowing what your body type is and how to dress it will alleviate the stress of shopping and buying clothes that are not flattering. For every body type, the goal is to create visual balance. When choosing clothing for your specific body type, you can camouflage what you do not like and flatter what you do.

One the first things I ask a new client is "What part of your body do you like?" I explain that we focus on the good—not the bad! Here is a general guideline to determine what your body type is and how to dress for it.

Hourglass: Larger/rounded bust and shoulders, defined waist, larger hips

Style goals. Emphasize your feminine curves and waist and draw attention up toward the face.

- Emphasize your waist by wearing clothes that narrow at the waist

- Flared trousers add volume below the knees and balance an hourglass figure

- Belts draw attention to your waist

- Wrap dresses cinch the waist and drape over your curves

- Draw eye attention up with V-neck tops

- Maintain visual balance on both the top and bottom

- Do not wear overly stiff fabrics—fabric should follow your curves

- Do not wear blousy tops or bulky clothes that hide your shape

Inverted Triangle: Broad shoulders, narrower hips/thighs, slim legs

Style goals. Emphasize your hips and waist, draw attention inward at shoulders toward the neck, and fill out the area below the waist with fullness or design detail.

- Add details like pockets, fabrics and patterns to the lower part of your body to balance out the upper half

- Wear full skirts

- Wear low necklines to slim and lengthen

- Do wear A-line dresses, halter dresses and full skirts

- Wear light-colored bottoms and dark-colored tops

- Do not wear shoulder pads or puffy sleeves that draw attention to the shoulders

- Avoid tops with shoulder details—we want to draw attention away from the shoulders

Triangle: Smaller shoulders and waist, average bust, larger hips

Style goals. Fill out the shoulders with soft fullness and design details, minimize the lower part of the body, and draw attention upward.

- Camouflage hips and thighs by wearing darker colors on the bottom and lighter colors on top

- Use wide collars—boat necks are great—to extend the shoulder line

- Wear accessories and designs that draw attention to the upper part of the body

- Do not wear tops that hit you directly at the hip

- Do not wear short skirts—they make you appear larger on the bottom

- Avoid halter style tops that drag the eyes down

Rectangle: Similar width shoulders, waist, hips and thighs

Style goals. Draw attention to the waist and up towards the face. Add curves by defining the shoulders and waist.

- Wear A-line skirts and pencil skirts

- Wear asymmetrical details on the top to draw the eye up

- Wear shoulder pads to help emphasize shoulders

- Hip length or longer jackets work best instead of jackets that hit at the widest part of the waist.

- Do not wear belts at the waist—go for low-slung belts

- Avoid very fitted clothes

- Avoid high turtleneck tops unless there is an additional design to distract the eye.

Tip for all body types: Keep prints and patterns in proportion to your body. If you are petite and small-boned, smaller prints and patterns work best. Medium size prints are better suited for women with medium size bodies. Larger bodies can wear large, bold prints and look fantastic. You always want to appear harmonious in prints and patterns so your clothes do not overwhelm you.

The Power of Color

"Mere color, unspoiled by meaning, and unallied with definite form, can speak to the soul in a thousand different ways."
—Oscar Wilde, Irish poet and dramatist

You can accomplish many different results based on the colors you wear. Colors that complement your skin, hair and eyes make you more appealing. You appear bright and alert, whereas the wrong colors for your skin tone can make you look tired and unhealthy. When you wear color near your face, light reflects the color upwards— this can cast either flattering tones or dark shadows, depending on the mix of color and your skin tone.

What does the color of your clothing tell the viewer?

Black. Black is considered a color of power and is worn by women who want to appear authoritative. In many cases, this color can make you appear thinner. Black communicates, "I am good at making my own decisions."

White. White is associated with purity and innocence. The message is, "I am clear, clean and reliable." This color is also symbolic of a sterile environment. Medical professionals wear white when they are working with patients. White clothes give the appearance of being refreshed.

Red. Red is a color associated with an increase in an individual's heart rate. It is the color of energy. In business, it means, "I am confident, and I want to be remembered." Red is a great color to wear when you want to appear powerful and in control.

Blue. Blue is a calming color and should be worn frequently. This color is symbolic of loyalty, peace and order. Many professionals typically wear this color to job interviews. A blue room increases productivity and work efficiency. Wearing blue means, "I am credible, trustworthy and capable."

Green. Green helps to calm the mind and provides a sense of reassurance. Hospitals also use this color in their waiting rooms to alleviate stress. The message when wearing green is, "I am bringing new fresh ideas to this presentation."

Purple. Purple is a color that signifies royalty. Purple lets people know you "think outside the box." People who wear purple appear to be regal, dignified, creative and sensitive.

Brown. Brown is associated with nature and stands for reliability. A lighter shade of brown conveys a sense of logic and intelligence. Wearing brown says, "I am reliable and dependable."

Guide to Dressing for Success on a Budget

Contrary to popular belief, dressing well does not take a lot of money. Not everyone can afford the latest fashions from designer stores. Knowing your own personal style and what level of dress you should be wearing are the keys to putting your professional wardrobe together. Shopping for the right clothes at inexpensive prices will be second nature.

Outlet shopping is a great way to start. Many times, you will find new styles in outlets because high-end department stores ordered too many items of clothing, and when the time comes to move the merchandise, it is sent to the outlet store. Some outlet malls carry the largest designer name brands in the world.

Discount stores like Ross,® Marshalls® or TJ Maxx® carry designer items at a fraction of the price of high-end retail stores. Target® carries designer items from Isaac Mizrahi® for considerably less than his couture line.

Great prices can also be found in consignment shops. Consignment shops carry designer brands at a fraction of their original cost because the seller no longer wants the garment. Many times the clothes are new with the tags still on them!

Start building your wardrobe with neutrals and gradually add color and accessories. Treat yourself to a high-end bag or an amazing pair of shoes, and people will assume your clothing is expensive as well!

A professional image is essential to everyone in the business world, and you do not have to have a CEO's paycheck to afford a great wardrobe. Know what is right for your body type, and you will have a successful shopping trip while sticking to your budget.

Are You Ready to Project a Polished Image?

If you are still a bit unsure about what to wear, study your corporate culture. Observe management to see what they are wearing and determine which level of dress your company prefers.

Always consider your audience. Think of the image you are trying to project and how you can incorporate the Style Scale into your situation. Always remember, people gravitate toward people who are well-dressed and confident.

Your professional image in the workplace shows that you understand the importance of your position and respect the people around you. A successful career requires continual planning and hard work. Dressing the part will help you take control and promote success in all that you do.

LAURA RUBELI
Image Consulting

(702) 767-5824

laura@laurarubeli.com.

www.laurarubeli.com

Laura Rubeli is a professional image consultant currently living and working in Las Vegas, Nevada. She is passionate about helping people look and feel their best, and she works with her clients to create a stylish wardrobe for both personal and professional success. Through private consultations, classes and corporate seminars, Laura is able to transform the way people feel about themselves by creating an image that positively reflects who they are inside.

Her early career in investment banking gave Laura the inside knowledge and background necessary to succeed in the corporate image consulting profession. She trained and received her certification through the Sterling Style Academy,® and she is a member of the Association of Image Consultants International. She works with several nonprofit organizations that provide clothing to disadvantaged women.

Laura has appeared nationally on radio and television, most notably on Lifetime's *The Balancing Act* and on ABC's *The Morning Blend*. She writes a quarterly column for *Las Vegas Woman Magazine* called "Fashion Fixations with Laura Rubeli." Her tips and expertise have been featured in the *Las Vegas Review Journal*, *More Magazine*, *FitBeautiful! Magazine* and many more.

Playing Win-Win

*How Women Can Pave the Way for
More Collaborative Leadership*

By Elizabeth Agnew, MS, ACC

Leadership needs to change. We are approaching a tipping point in our society where we need a new set of tools and principles to effectively solve the toughest problems facing us today. Women are particularly equipped to bring a new way of leading into common business practice.

Jeremy Rifkin, in his book *The Empathic Civilization,* published by Jeremy Tarcher in 2009, underscored the increasing trend toward empathy and the rise of consciousness. "We are actually soft-wired for sociability, attachment, affection, companionship. . . ." Our first drive is *to belong.*

Rifkin's book is one of many recent publications emphasizing the importance of feminine qualities for great leadership. Women have a powerful ability to empathize, handle complex incoming information and demonstrate a natural drive to collaborate. As a woman, you are poised to make a huge difference by bringing leadership principles and practices into the 21st century.

What does it mean to be a "collaborative leader?" Stop for a minute and think of your own definition of this.

Collaboration is a nebulous term that surfaces frequently but has little substance. Despite the difficulty of defining it, you know when you experience it. Because collaboration is an essential element of leadership, this chapter will give you a greater understanding of what it means to lead collaboratively, so you can become a more effective leader. You will also discover a set of principles to guide you and a better understanding of the changes you can make to overcome leadership challenges.

"We must understand that we lose capacity and in fact create more chaos when we insist on hierarchy, roles, and command and control leadership."
—Margaret J. Wheatley, American author

An Authentic Path to Powerful, Effective Leadership

Do the traditional forms of command-and-control leadership you have been taught create internal conflict or feelings of inauthenticity? Have heavy-handed leadership approaches left you feeling less powerful rather than more?

The command-and-control leadership style that dominates the workplace culture simply does not work. This leadership structure is based on a chain-of-command model designed for the repetitive, well-defined tasks of the industrial era. Today's economy is no longer built around manufacturing and consumer goods; it feeds on knowledge and information. People simply do not want to be told what to do anymore—not that they ever did. This discrepancy in the work people do and the way people lead is made starkly evident by the October 2006 issue of *Gallup Management Journal*'s "Employee Engagement Index" which says that 71 percent of employees are disengaged in their jobs!

Imagine leadership styles along a feminine-masculine spectrum. Stereotypical masculine leadership qualities are actions such as making decisions, giving clear direction, discerning between ideas and, of course, driving toward a goal. Feminine leadership qualities include being inquisitive and inclusive, supporting creativity, nourishing new ideas and allowing something transformational to emerge. Traditional leadership most often sits on the masculine end of the spectrum.

To be effective, your leadership style needs to include *both* ends of the feminine-masculine spectrum. You need a balanced framework for leadership in order to navigate the knowledge economy and address the complex problems of today.

The COS™ Fundamentals

This section will give you the fundamental building blocks of the Collaborative Operating System™ (COS), a way of working designed to cross the chasms of structure and fluidity, of discipline and creativity, and of individual and collective interests.

Effective leadership strategy focuses on solving specific problems by building ownership with—and alignment among—all stakeholders about the problem and the steps required to solve it. Building ownership and alignment is easier when the distinction is made between what you are doing and how you are doing it.

Identify the problem you are solving. Collaborative leaders begin all initiatives with one simple, powerful question, "What problem are we trying to solve?" A "problem" is defined as any situation you want to change. Answering this question with your team will build ownership and alignment around your strategic agenda.

> *"In a crisis if I had only an hour I'd spend the first 50 minutes defining the problem and the last 10 minutes solving it."*
> —Albert Einstein, German-American physicist
> and Nobel Prize winner

By identifying the problem, you do three important things.

First, you determine that a business problem exists and the effort is legitimate. Solving real business problems is the primary goal of leadership.

Second, you ensure that your team believes the problem is worth solving and can be solved. People will truly commit themselves to a project only when they believe it is worth trying to solve.

Third, identifying the problem as a team creates high commitment to solving the problem. When you create ownership and alignment around the problem, you can then gain the team's ownership and alignment around the solution

Involve all stakeholders. It is important to have the right people involved from the beginning. Even though it can feel like more work for you to involve more people, it is ultimately a shortcut. If you leave out people who are truly stakeholders, the results you generate will not be effective.

Recently, I was planning a reunion for my high school graduating class in collaboration with the class president. We thought we were planning an event people wanted—a barbeque at the local beach. A few people voiced complaints about the venue, but we thought they were a minority. Then I received a message from someone who lived in my hometown who said people there did not like how the event was shaping up and felt we had not put a lot of thought into it.

While I felt defensive about this at first, I was able to see the root problem: We had no local representation in the planning and decision making. I was 3,000 miles away in California, and our class president was 500 miles away in Washington, D.C.! We were leaving out a key constituency group who clearly had a stake in the event's success.

We responded by inviting the friend who spoke up to our next planning call. Her email to us showed she was committed and willing to help, and she had much easier access to local information than we did. In the end, we pulled off a great event and let everyone know we could not have done it without her—or them. Local graduates thanked *us* for our hard work. Everybody won!

Nothing destroys trust more than leaving a stakeholder group out of the process. In the case of my high school reunion, we were able to bring key stakeholders in and repair trust before it was too late.

Create ownership and alignment. Traditional leaders use power and authority to get work done. Collaborative leaders use the principles of ownership and alignment. Ownership is the degree to which people believe or feel that a process, decision or outcome is theirs. Alignment is the degree to which people see and understand the problem, goal or process in the same way. Ownership is getting everyone in the same boat. Alignment is getting everyone rowing in the same direction.

People know when something is theirs. Is the chair you are sitting in yours? It becomes a little trickier when you are assessing your ownership of an intangible object. How about your most recent meeting at work? Was that your meeting or were you just showing up at someone else's meeting?

> *"Times of upheaval require not just more leadership but more leaders. People at all organizational levels, whether anointed or self-appointed, must be empowered to share leadership responsibilities."*
> —Rosalynn Carter, former first lady of the United States

The shift in your emphasis from power and authority to ownership and alignment will create leaders at every level. If you lead using ownership and alignment, people will start to step up more fully because sharing ideas and information is an advantage in a collaborative organization.

You can be an effective leader by becoming proficient in the creation and maintenance of ownership and alignment. If you can build joint ownership for work products and processes, the rest falls in place because people take care of what they own.

Distinguish between process and content. In order for a team to *work* together towards a common goal, they must have a way to *stay* together as they work to reach that goal. This means they must agree on the goal (the *what*) and also the path to get there (the *how*). *Content* is the *what*, and *process* is the *how*. As a collaborative leader, you must build ownership and alignment around both process and content.

In order for someone to own and align with both content and process, he or she must be skilled at distinguishing between the two types of information. Failing to distinguish between process and content makes it harder to keep your team together, which is necessary for collaboration!

A quick story from a client team meeting I recently facilitated illustrates the need to differentiate between content and process. The team's meeting agenda included a discussion that answered the question: What questions did your direct reports raise about the new health care coverage, and what were those questions, if any? During that discussion, one team member, who happened to be pregnant, asked about how the coverage was changing. Another team member answered, and the group was now off track. They were talking about the coverage itself, which was the *what*, when they had planned to discuss *how* the coverage had been received by their direct reports. My ability to make the distinction between the *what* and the *how* enabled me to get the meeting back on track.

As you can see, the Collaborative Operating System is a way of working that goes to the heart of win-win and enables workers to engage in ways that serve themselves, each other and the organization simultaneously.

How to Lead Collaboratively for Real Results

Women leaders face workplace problems today that are more complex than ever before. Prescriptive, "do this, do that" approaches will not serve. Principle-based leadership creates a foundation on which you can lead a team through any situation. Although the Collaborative Operating System contains concrete tools to implement its principles, it starts with your paradigm as a leader.

Play a win-win game. Collaboration cannot exist outside of a win-win culture. This culture starts with your attitude as a leader. It takes personal work to operate with a win-win attitude, and it starts with being clear about what constitutes a win for you. Get in touch with what you want, be authentic and stick to it.

Sometimes women in leadership positions believe that if they are too nice, people will think they are pushovers, and if they are tough, people will not want to work with them. Let go of this type of thinking. Being nice and tough are not polar opposites. Instead, practice seeing these qualities co-exist. This is one way to find your masculine-feminine leadership balance.

Win-win outcomes require you to overcome either-or mentalities. Roger Martin, dean of the Rotman School of Management, University of Toronto, put it this way in *The Opposable Mind,* published in 2009 by Harvard Business Press: "The leaders I have studied share at least one trait . . . .They have the predisposition and the capacity to hold to diametrically opposing ideas in their heads. And then, without panicking or simply settling for one alternative or the other, they're able to produce a synthesis that is superior to either opposing idea." This ability, which takes consideration, courage and patience, is fundamental to a win-win skill set.

Embrace emotions. As a woman, you have an advantage here. You can start seeing your feminine ability to embrace emotion as an asset, not a liability, for effective leadership.

Tuning in emotionally to team members can give you valuable clues to their levels of ownership or alignment. Low ownership might mean an employee will not treat the project or goal as carefully as necessary, or their work might be headed in the wrong direction. On the other hand, this team member might see things differently from others in a way that could actually benefit the team in some way. If you sense someone's ownership or alignment is low, engage that person in a way that repairs it.

If you are in touch with them, your emotions can serve as a weathervane for the stickiest of leadership situations. Your emotions can also be the messenger of your intuition. Harnessed constructively, the wisdom contained within emotions can benefit the tough conversations you have to have with those around you in order to maintain or repair trust.

Reframe your role. As you imagine yourself to be a powerful leader, the picture may come with unarticulated assumptions, judgments or beliefs about your role. Is your role as a leader to delegate, motivate, inspire, redirect, dictate or teach? What does your role include, and what is outside the boundaries of your leadership?

As a collaborative leader, think of your role as one of coach and facilitator. Your job is not to control but to guide and empower. A facilitator is someone who makes it easier for others to do their jobs effectively—someone who enables work to be accomplished.

With collaborative leadership, teams do not need to rely on your authority to get work done, and you no longer pose a bottleneck to work flow. Even if you are in a position of authority, relying on that authority to convince others to perform is draining and ineffective. Ownership and alignment among the team is how good work gets done—it is your job as a collaborative leader to build and maintain these important qualities.

In the February 2006 issue of *Harvard Business Review,* thought leader Gary Hamel wrote about the imperative of management innovation: "If you want to build an organization that unshackles the human spirit, you're going to need some decidedly unbureaucratic management principles."

Leading with principles from the Collaborative Operating System will enable you to rise above bureaucracy to connect and engage people by facilitating truly self-governing teams. This comprehensive win-win approach to leading in the twenty-first century will bring the superior results your leadership style is capable of achieving!

ELIZABETH AGNEW, MS, ACC
Integrative Leadership Strategies, LLC

*Lead with win-win and get
sustainable results to complex problems*

(415) 401-7822

liz@integrative-leadership.com

www.integrative-leadership.com

Elizabeth Agnew is a certified coach, specializing in leadership development and collaboration. She holds a bachelor's degree from Cornell University and a master's degree from Stanford University. She became a coach in 2006 to serve individuals and organizations that want to make a bigger difference and need leadership development to do so.

As president of Integrative Leadership Strategies, LLC, Liz is a trainer, consultant and coach. She works closely with leaders who want to lead more effectively, help their teams work together more strategically and bring together disparate stakeholders to more competently solve complex problems.

Liz's mission is to make the workplace a sanctuary for learning and truth. She provides tools and resources for a more organized and effective change strategy and offers guidance on operating collaboratively to achieve better results. She shows her clients how to lead more sustainably, strategically and consciously. Her clients have strong visions for positive change and have included individuals and teams from Genentech,® Hewlett Packard,® The City of Atlanta, Sun Microsystems,® State Farm Insurance® and the California Public Utilities Commission, among others.

Maximizing Your Everyday Moments of Truth
Savvy Strategies for Verbal Communication
By Ann Kelley

A *moment of truth* is that moment of contact when someone forms an impression of you. It does not matter whether this occurs in person, in writing or via telecommunications. The result is the same. Savvy women leaders recognize the power of these moments and the impact they can have on their career.

Most opinions about you are formed based on how you look and how you sound. This does not mean *what* you say is unimportant. It means that *how* you say it could have a more lasting impact.

You have been told for years not to judge a book by its cover. Have you ever been told not to judge a book by its contents? No. The truth is words have power. Words can create interest, curiosity and imagery. Words can also hurt. Therefore, if every interaction you have with another individual has the possibility of being a moment of truth, it would be savvy for you to develop verbal strategies to help master everyday moments. Even harsh messages can be viewed as constructive if communicated with wisdom and grace.

"Communication is the real work of leadership."
—Nitin Nohria, Indian professor and dean of Harvard Business School

Communication and Everyday Moments of Truth

Communication only occurs when the message you deliver is received in the spirit and way you intended. Some of the most common interactions with others leave lasting impressions. How often are these impressions not what you intended? You simply do not know.

If you are like most women leaders, you may find yourself in as many as twenty moments of truth every day. Each of these interactions might have as many as five or more people involved. This adds up to a significant number of opportunities for you to be impactful and memorable.

What Is Verbal Savviness?

Savvy communication techniques help you maximize your verbal impression in a way that conveys authenticity and builds credibility and impact.

The average person sends more than 200 messages a day via verbal, written or behavioral interactions. Most of these messages are up for interpretation. Do people hear what you say or are your messages and meanings lost in the moment? Whether you are sending an email, leaving a message or talking face to face, language is an imperfect communication tool.

Your verbal impression is a combination of what you say and how you say it. These elements are critical to your success as a savvy leader and are a significant part of your professional image. You may be able to look the part, but you have to be able to speak the part as well. For more about your physical presentation, see "Success Appeal" by Karen Solomon on page 87.

Savvy Verbal Strategies

Use clear, specific and concise statements. The savvy leader knows that the power of clarity has a direct connection to the power of meaning. For example, saying "thank you" for a job well done is not as meaningful as saying, "Thank you for the way you handled those difficult calls today. I particularly liked the way you showed patience and empathy to our customers."

Avoid competing monologues. It is natural to be thinking while people are talking. When thinking turns to what you will say next, your listening stops, and your monologues begin competing with the other person's communication.

Minimize the use of having to clarify meaning. If you need to put a further definition into the conversation, there is a good chance you are not being clear and concise in the first place.

Moments of Truth: What You Say

The savvy leader utilizes moments of truth to create influence, build relationships and promote themselves and the work they do. For many of you, the idea of self-promotion may seem egotistical. However, if you are not promoting yourself, then who is? Embrace the opportunities you have to build credibility with others.

Developing verbal savviness can be as easy as creating new and innovative approaches to things you already do on a regular basis—such as introducing yourself and your elevator speech.

Introducing yourself. Picture yourself sitting in a room full of people as each person goes around and introduces himself or herself. You stifle a yawn. During most introductions like these, people do not listen to the introductions. Instead, they think about what they are going to say when their turn comes.

Use your introduction as a way to engage in a conversation with someone later. This is a great opportunity to highlight what you do and the impact you have. You can set yourself apart from others by focusing on the benefits of working with you. People will seek you out just to find out more.

Basically, hook them and leave them wanting more. Which of the following introductions would create more interest in people? Number One or Number Two?

1. Hello, my name is Ann Kelley. I am the president of MBD Training Consultants. Our goal is to develop more, better or different skills in individuals.

2. Hello, my name is Ann. I specialize in taking people outside of their comfort zone to show them how powerful they can be once they get there.

The first example is boring and would not likely prompt someone to seek me out unless they were interested in skill development. The second example creates a level of mystery and intrigue. People are not sure what you are talking about and that creates interest. Here is how you can do this:

• Focus on results or impact, not on vague statements. The goal is to have someone want to learn more, not have him or her say, "What was that about?"

• Believe what you are saying. You will not have cue cards to help you. You need to know it and feel it. Write and practice it until it becomes second nature.

The elevator speech. An elevator speech is your thirty seconds of fame. You are in the spotlight, whether you sought the opportunity out or someone sought you out.

An elevator speech does not always happen at or in an elevator. You could be waiting at a coffee cart, sitting in your cubicle or running into someone in a hallway.

An elevator speech is designed to give an update, set up a future appointment or simply promote you. The elevator speech is another example of a moment of truth that has the potential to create a lasting impression.

Opportunities to use an elevator speech may occur when someone says:

• "I have not seen you in ages. What have you been up to?"

• "Can you give me an update on the XYZ project?"

• "I don't believe we've met. Who are you and what is it you do?"

It can also be seen as an extended introduction. It creates interest by utilizing a hook statement, and it creates validation by expressing results or evidence. An elevator speech may feel like you are selling something. You are. You are selling yourself.

An elevator speech for someone who has never met you might sound like this:

"Hello my name is Ann. I specialize in taking people outside of their comfort zone to show them how powerful they can be once they get there. I believe everyone should experience this sensation. Just yesterday, I was working with a group of senior leaders during a presentation workshop. Each one of them commented on how much improvement they made once they were willing to step outside their individual comfort zone. I would love to set up some time to tell you more about these experiences and how it could benefit your team."

If a colleague asks about the update on the XYZ project, that elevator speech might sound like this:

"When we last spoke, you mentioned the implementation plan needed to be completed by month end. I am excited to share with you that we are on target. In fact, just yesterday, we had a project team meeting, and all statuses were green. I would be happy to set up some time to review the project plan in more detail with you."

No matter what kind of elevator speech you need to make, here are some tips for making them highly effective.

• Use the first sentence to create interest or hook your audience in. Telling someone that you have been busy is not memorable. What hook could you use right now to interest someone?

• Communicate your point of view. Do not be afraid to express how you feel about the particular topic. Do not be afraid to show enthusiasm.

• Provide evidence or examples that are easily understood and directly connected to your topic. If you are going to use personal experience as your evidence, make sure it is current. No one wants to hear what you did five years ago.

• Be assertive about setting an appointment for later. Asking someone *if* he or she would like to set up an appointment could end with a negative response.

• Be ready at all times with your basic introduction elevator speech. You never know who you will see at the elevator.

Moments of Truth: How You Say It

How you say things can be just as important as what you say. In some instances, it can be more important. I am sure that you have been in situations where the words were right, but how something was said gave the message a completely different meaning than what was intended.

When people listen, they do not just listen. They think about:

- What is being said
- Whether or not they believe you
- How they feel about your message
- What they can do with the information
- What is in it for them
- How they will make this work

The verbal components of how your message is being evaluated include:

- Volume
- Pace
- Tone and inflection
- Filler words and sounds

The verbal components of how your message is being evaluated include:

Volume. How loud you speak depends on the setting and purpose of your communication. If you speak too loudly, you could be perceived as aggressive. If you speak too softly, you could be perceived as meek.

- Speak up. You are not speaking as loud as it seems to you. Remember, your ears are fairly close to your mouth. What you hear is not the same as what your listener hears.
- Breathe. The result is a stronger projection of your voice.

Pace. Managing your pace is an important component of your verbal impression. If you speak too fast, your message might be lost. If you speak too slowly, people will lose interest. Here are some tips for managing pace.

- Embrace the power of the pause and do not be afraid of silence. A couple of seconds of silence is just enough time to let your listener catch up.

- Record yourself to establish a baseline of how you speak. This will help you get a sense of what you sound like and where you can improve.

- Vary your pacing. If your message has portions that are exciting, use a quicker pace. When the tone is more serious or contemplative, slow down. Use the middle ground of pacing for all other times.

> *"Sometimes there is a greater lack of communication in facile talking than in silence."*
> —Faith Baldwin, American author

Tone and inflection. Your voice has a wide range of power that can be conveyed with tone and inflection. By varying tone and inflection, you express emotions and energy and add meaning to your words. That is the good news.

The bad news is this: Tone and inflection can also create the wrong meaning and change someone's understanding of your message. We have all experienced this dynamic. You are talking to someone, and their words do not match their tone and inflection.

If you are telling people you are excited about something but are conveying the message with low volume and a monotonous tone, you risk being unbelievable. Here is how to use tone and inflection to convey the right message.

- Practice important messages *aloud*. It is easy to create incredible results in your head, only to find that when you say the words aloud, they do not come out the way you intended.

- Decide which words you want to emphasize and practice different tones. Telling someone, "I have a great opportunity for you" can take on several meanings depending on which word you decide to place your emphasis.

- Record yourself reading a book to hear how you sound. The variations in tone and inflection you hear are the same ones that others hear.

- Call your own phone and listen to your voicemail message. Does it convey confidence and energy? If not, re-record it.

Filler words. Filler words are annoying. No one has ever heard someone who used a lot of filler and thought, "Wow, that was great." The overuse of filler words or sounds can significantly impact your credibility—even in casual conversations. Filler words can make you appear nervous when you are not.

What is a filler word? A filler word is anything you use to bridge your thoughts. It can be something as simple as "umm," which is used as an expression of doubt or hesitation. Doubt? Hesitation? This is not the impression you want to convey when interacting with others.

Any word that is used in excess can be considered a filler word. Other common filler words are "so," "and," "but," "uh," "you know" and "like."

Let's not forget corporate lingo that turns into filler words. I recently heard a presenter uses the word "strategy" or "strategic" fourteen times in the first ten minutes of their talk. How did I know? My attention was drawn early on to the repetition and I am a counter. If your audience is counting, they are not listening.

Here are some simple steps for eliminating and minimizing the use of filler words.

- **Focus your eyes on one person at a time.** By speaking to one person at a time, you will minimize the stimulation your brain sees. Too much stimulation causes your body to react in a way that may create the illusion you are afraid or nervous. If you move your eyes rapidly from one person to another, your pace of speaking will quicken, resulting in the appearance of filler words.

- **Build in natural pauses when speaking.** When speaking to a group, a natural pause is helpful as you move your eyes from one person to another. When speaking one-on-one, a natural pause is as easy as taking a breath. The silence allows your listener(s) to catch up and allows you to gather your thoughts.

- **Record yourself speaking to determine your filler of choice.** Most people do not even realize how often they use filler words, and that they use the same one over and over.

Applying Savvy Verbal Strategies

As a savvy leader, embrace every interaction as a moment of truth. By recognizing the value and impact of your verbal impression, you will be better prepared to influence others, build credibility and ensure your message is received in the spirit and way it was intended.

Executing several new savvy verbal techniques at once can be overwhelming. Start small. Determine which strategy to begin with and practice until it becomes a part of your skill set. Recording yourself is the easiest way to identify which strategy needs your attention first.

Now is the time to step outside your communication comfort zone and discover how powerful you can be. By implementing these savvy strategies to improve your verbal communication, you can ensure that you are maximizing every moment of truth.

ANN KELLEY
MBD Training Consultants

Developing More, Better or Different Skills

(877) 572-5959

annkelley@mbdtraining.com

www.mbdtraining.com

Ann's passion for helping others grow is a hallmark of her success. Since 1990, Ann has had a highly successful career. She launched MBD Training Consultants and the MBD Experience in 2004 with a very simple goal—create an environment that is safe, fun and focused on helping individuals and businesses see the power in doing something more, better or different.

Whether it is a training seminar, a speaking engagement or one-on-one coaching, as a top expert in leadership and professional development, her client engagements are focused on providing enriching learning experiences that equip participants to achieve greater success. Ann's clients range from large companies with international presence to small nonprofit organizations.

Ann has an extensive human resources, change management and project management background, which allows her to maximize skill development independent of the industry or organizational level of participants. Her ability to customize learning solutions and her unique style of engaging all levels of learners in a safe and fun learning environment is superior. Her clients range from large financial, insurance and IT companies with international presence to small nonprofit organizations.

Influence—How to Create It, How to Keep It

By Caterina Rando, MA, MCC

The longer I am in business, the more I realize whom you know and who knows you are the tip of the iceberg for having your network work for you. Cultivating a network on and offline means consciously creating a pool of contacts from which you draw clients, resources, referrals and opportunities.

The savvy leader knows that networking is only a small part of having influence with the people you know. Being well-known, being popular or being recognized does not mean you have influence. After all, what good is it to have everyone know your name and your face if they do not know what you do, or how respected you are in your field, or how smart or reliable you are? What is far worse is if everyone knows you and seeks to avoid you when they see you because you never stop talking about yourself, or no one recommends or refers others to you because you have a reputation for being rude?

Influence is the ability to affect others, to impact their thoughts and actions toward your desired outcome. Influence equals ease in creating what you want in your professional and personal life. Cultivating influence with the people in your network is really where your attention will reap the most reward. What matters is who trusts you, respects you, remembers you, has a deep understanding of what you do and wants to help you. When you can create all this with one of your contacts, you now have influence. Influence and leadership go hand in hand— *your* ability to influence others is a key component of how effective a leader you can become.

Without influence, whatever you are doing that involves other people is harder—getting clients is harder, getting people to listen to you is harder, and even getting your phone calls returned is harder. Everything is harder without influence.

I want you to enjoy a life where exciting opportunities come to you regularly, where every time you walk into a room—a boardroom, an exhibit hall or your local coffee shop—people know your name and are thrilled to see you. I want you to have a life where you get through to other influential people when you call them, where all your invitations are accepted and your potential clients and project colleagues say a resounding yes to working with you even before they meet you.

That is the kind of life influential leaders enjoy every day and that is what I want for you. Here is my equation for building influence, and I encourage you to embrace immediately.

Visibility + Value + Consistency = Influence

Visibility is simply showing up online and offline. A product brand often has to be seen several times by someone before they will purchase a product. The same is sometimes true for people who are cultivating influence. When people see you in a variety of places and situations, you have different opportunities to connect—this builds influence. How can you be more visible and more influential?

Value occurs when you give, share or assist someone with something that they find useful. You can let them know about a resource that can save their company money, tell them about a book you think they will enjoy, or have an authentic conversation where they feel really seen and heard by you. These are just a few examples of providing value. Where can you provide value to people in your network that also enhances your influence?

Consistency of good behavior is key for building influence with others. This includes consistently being on time, meeting deadlines, being responsive and being open and receptive to ideas. Are you consistent in your professional life? Where could you improve consistency and, thus, influence?

Remember the Visibility + Value + Consistency = Influence equation as you read the rest of this chapter. This is the foundation of your plan to cultivate influence.

Sometimes, influence is bestowed simple because of position, as is the case with a company CEO or elected official. Many people bestow influence on the wealthy or "the beautiful people." This kind of influence is outside of what I will focus on here. Follow the strategies in this chapter to create more influence starting today, in whatever position you hold, with whatever economic level you enjoy. These ideas will build your influence with everyone you already know and everyone you will meet in the future. You can use them to become the influential leader you are meant to be.

Be Positive

A smile looks good on everyone. It conveys welcome and says, "I am happy to talk with you." It is the easiest way to be friendly and approachable.

When you have a positive disposition, people are much more likely to connect with you. Here is something you probably know from psychology that absolutely applies to building influence. The biggest predictor of future behavior is past behavior. If the last time someone met you on an elevator or saw you at an event, you were complaining about something, he or she would be less likely to reach out to you again because the last impression of you was negative. Your past behavior will influence their ideas about your future behavior.

Be positive, do not complain and do not criticize yourself or others. If a smile makes everyone more beautiful, a complaint or gossip makes everyone ugly. People want to associate with, invite and recommend people whom they want to be around.

Demonstrate a Genuine Interest in Others

Early in my career, I attended a business event with one of my mentors. I was impressed when she walked up to people she did not know, smiled, put out her hand and said, "Hi, I am Kimberly. I have not met you yet."

Everyone she approached responded with a smile and a handshake. They gave her their names and conversation ensued. I use this everywhere. I follow up the introductions by asking a couple of interested, open-ended questions about the person. My favorite question is to ask them what is the newest or most exciting thing going on with them or what is the best thing that has happened to them lately. People love to answer these questions because it gives them an opportunity to shine and lets them talk about whatever they like.

People will find you charming, smart and interesting—even if you hardly say anything. This is what I call *influence with ease.*

Once you have met someone, you have to get to know him or her and, if your first interaction was a positive one, you begin to build trust. Build on that first meeting by doing a few simple things. Remember someone's name and friend them on Facebook® or LinkedIn® right away, so you will have their picture. Immediately follow up on any action you agreed to take. Send a nice-to-meet-you note—it is done so rarely these days, and definitely serves to build influence for you and makes a great follow-up to a strong first impression.

Have a Strong Personal Brand

Your behavior, your presence, your personality and your professional image have to be consistent in order to convey the impression you want to make. Your personal brand is not just the colors you use in your business and your tagline. Your appearance, your behavior and your communication are all part of your personal brand. You may have had your colors done, worked with an image professional and have a great smile that makes you approachable. None of this matters if you show up only fifty percent of the time to a committee meeting, are always late and never offer to help. The people on the committee will perceive you as unreliable at best, flaky at worst, and you will have no influence with any of them.

Give attention to your personal brand. One of my favorite personal branding exercises as it relates to influence is to write down six or seven words that you want people to say about you. Put those words in front of you in your office and read them every day. Make sure everything you say and do, and everything that represents you, such as a website, receptionist or voicemail message, reflects these words. For example, the words I have posted in front of me in my office are "honest, positive, warm, approachable, expert, dynamic and excellent." I make sure everything that happens in my business reflects these words. I make it easy for people to connect with me, and my team and I are always striving for better client care. I am always looking for how we can improve what we do and how we do it. This also means that if something has worked for other businesses, and it is not consistent with my personal brand, I will not do it because it would dilute my influence in the marketplace. For more on enhancing your personal brand see Karen Solomon's "Success Appeal" on page 87 and Laura Rubeli's chapter "The Savvy Woman's Guide to a Polished Image" on page 99.

Cultivate Community, Connection and Camaraderie

You have influence with people who know you, trust you, like you and think highly of you and or your skills. It can sometimes be impossible to meet and get to know the people with whom you want to cultivate influence. You can overcome this challenge by consciously implementing some fun, social and professional community-building plans. Ask yourself what you can do to consistently and effectively build your relationships and cultivate camaraderie in all areas of your life. Here are some ideas to get you started.

Invite people to go where you are going. This is a great way to let people know that you want to get to know them better. Whenever you are going to a conference, a seminar, a charity luncheon or even a yoga class, think about whom you want to get to know better who would appreciate an invitation. Invite several people to join you at once, and they will start by telling each other how wonderful you are. This definitely helps with influence building.

Host personal events. Many influential people hold an annual backyard barbeque or a holiday event, or put together a group to participate in a walkathon followed by a party. Note, I said, "annual event." Consistency over time creates results. One event is good, and a strategy of consistently hosting events is far better.

Host online business and professional events. A few years ago, I developed a new niche with image consultants for my business consulting and training practice. In order to get "in front" of as many image professionals as possible, I started to host free, information-packed teleclasses. This brought me clients from four continents that I have never met and built my reputation as a business-building expert in that industry. This is an easy way to cultivate influence. Hosting webinars is equally effective.

Host offline business and professional events. There is nothing better than inviting potential clients and people in your field to your own events. This could be an evening workshop or a reception to celebrate the release of your new book, an anniversary reception or an open house. Any reason to invite people to be with you at an event you are hosting is a great idea. In most cases, you have more influence with people after you have met them in person.

Start your own large or small association or group. When you are the founder and leader of a group, you receive some "insta-influence." If you want to be a part of a group of professionals that learn about building wealth—start one. If you want to get to know people who are in the same industry as you in your city—start a group. Start a mastermind group, or start a group of people who raise money for a charitable cause you care about. This is a great way to build your network, hone your leadership skills and, of course, create influence.

Return emails and phone calls promptly. I know this is tough with our super busy lives, and it is more important than ever. Because the people in your network know you receive a lot of calls and emails, you make a greater impression when you get right back to people. It shows you care.

Connect in online communities. Reach out on a daily or weekly basis to people you want to meet or whom you already know and have not yet connected with online. Sometimes, when I travel to another city for business, I invite my Facebook friends and LinkedIn connections to join me for a networking reception. This is a great way to make your online connections count. These receptions have resulted in new clients and opportunities.

Be Generous

Being generous feels great. I learned this first-hand because my mother has always been a happy, generous person. She was an elementary school teacher for many years, and she often stayed late to work with students who needed extra help. She gave supplies to children who could not afford them and always greeted both students and teachers by name and with a smile. She was the most influential teacher in her school without even trying.

There is an Italian saying she used as a guiding principle in life that I want you to embrace: *Fa bene, e disricordare,* which translates into "do good and forget about it."

I was shocked recently when I heard a celebrity say she keeps track of all the kind things she does for someone, so she can remind them of it when she needs something. This is ridiculous. Do good and forget about it. The law of reciprocity will keep track for you.

There are five unique ways to be generous, five different ways to show someone you genuinely care about them and want to help. You can give them your time, your money, words of appreciation or encouragement, gifts and your contacts. Be generous with all of these. Pick up the check, buy the fundraising candy bar, accept the invitation for coffee someone extends to ask your advice. Do everything you can to connect people with the people they want to meet.

When thinking about being generous with your time, this can also mean being generous with your listening or being generous with advice or guidance. Another way to be generous is to invite and include people in a meeting or event you think would benefit them. I often invite people as my guests to my live trainings because I know they will get value from it. This creates goodwill and cultivates great relationships.

I already shared a favorite, generous thing I do is to invite people to go where I am going. This combines one idea from above with being generous. If I am going to a luncheon, a networking event or a workshop, I invite several people whom I know would enjoy attending. Creating influence is magnified when you have a table full of people who all know you and do not yet know each other. The first thing they do is talk about you and how fabulous you are!

Communicating Your Needs

Once you have strong rapport with people, make requests of them for business or contacts. If you ask people to hire you as soon as they meet you, you will probably see hesitation on their part and sometimes even resentment. It is naive to expect people to use your services or refer others to you until you have created influence with them.

Influence is cultivated over time. Look at the people in your network. Have you created good rapport with them? Do you stay in regular contact so they remember you? Are you generous? If so, it is time to think about how you can use your influence to grow your business by asking people to refer others to work with you. If not, get working on what you have learned here. The more influence you have, the more your business will thrive, and the more what *you* want will come *to you with ease.*

CATERINA RANDO, MA, MCC
Business Strategist, Speaker, Publisher

Making you and your business thrive

(415) 668-4535

cat@caterinarando.com

www.caterinarando.com

www.caterinaspeaks.com

www.thrivebooks.com

Caterina Rando's mission is to show women entrepreneurs how to build thriving businesses. She is a sought-after speaker, business strategist and author of the national bestseller, *Learn to Power Think,* from Chronicle Books. Caterina is co-author of *Direct Selling Power, Incredible Business* and *Make Your Connections Count.* She is also featured as a success expert in several other leading business books including: *Build It Big, Get Clients Now* and *Get Slightly Famous.*

Since 1993, Caterina has been providing consulting, training and solutions to ensure women entrepreneurs succeed. Through her Business Breakthrough Summit and Sought After Speaker Summit, she and her team show women how to become recognized as experts, think and plan strategically and significantly grow their revenue. She is also the founder of THRIVE Publishing,™ a company that publishes multi-author books, including this book, for experts who want to share their message with a greater market.

Caterina holds a bachelor of science degree in organizational behavior and a master of arts degree in life transitions counseling psychology. She is a certified personal and professional coach (CPPC) and a master certified coach (MCC), the highest designation awarded by the International Coaching Federation.®

Media Training—Pay Now or Pay Later

What You Do Not Know Can Hurt You!

By Malena Cunningham

Media training is the one class that is not taught in graduate school to future business owners, executives and leaders. However, in today's 24/7 news environment, top leaders must be prepared to meet the press at all times, whether a crisis comes or not. Good media training will affect public opinion of you and your business, which, in turn, can positively affect your bottom line. On the other hand, failing to handle media exposure appropriately can be disastrous for your business.

As a former television news reporter and anchor, I have covered a number of high profile stories that thrust a business or corporate executive into a negative spotlight. I observed how these executives handled or mishandled the media and how this directly affected their businesses.

> *"There cannot be a stressful crisis next week,*
> *my schedule is full already."*
> —Henry Kissinger, German-born former
> United States secretary of state

On August 6, 2007, the American people were glued to their televisions. Nine workers were trapped underground following a mine collapse in Utah. As days turned into a long nightmare for their families, Bob Murray, president of Murray Industries,° which owned the Crandall Canyon mine near Huntingdon, Utah, stepped into the spotlight to face the media. Two days after the accident, Murray held a press conference, which was covered live on CNN.° It was not his first time addressing what allegedly caused the mine collapse or what the company was doing to rescue the miners. This time, however, when Murray spoke, people gasped.

The more Murray talked, the worse it got. He rambled, chastised the media and contradicted the facts regarding what may have caused the mining accident. He gave conflicting details on the latest rescue efforts. This media mess appears on YouTube,° and you can still see it today. Media mistakes go around the world in a split second thanks to the Internet, and those mistakes live on long after the crisis is over. All the while, the public is forming its own opinion on the crisis and the company.

Contrast this scenario with another CEO, Debbi Fields, the founder of Mrs. Fields° Cookies. In the 1980s, an anonymous chain letter was circulated that claimed a customer bought the original recipe for the famous chocolate chip cookie from Mrs. Fields. The letter suggested the recipe had been sold for a small sum and encouraged anyone who received a copy to send it to all his or her friends. To this day, no one knows who wrote or circulated the letter that could have ruined a multi-million dollar business. Debbi Fields was proactive when this crisis hit. She went to the media and to her customers to dispel the letter. A sign was posted on the doors of all of her cookie stores denouncing the letter and its allegations that her cookie recipe had been sold. This was a proactive, positive media response by a corporate leader.

By the time the Utah mining disaster happened, I was retired from the news business and working as a media relations consultant at the company I founded. I watched that live CNN press conference with Bob Murray and could not believe what I was hearing. The manner with which he handled the media was a perfect case study for several of my corporate clients. I still use it as an example to show everything that can and will go wrong when you face the media without training and without a plan.

Most of the clients I worked with at that time were in the middle of their own media firestorm. They knew how they got there, but they did not know how to get out. The answer was usually simple. Those making the decisions were *reacting* to negative media coverage and not being *proactive.* They did not understand how to make the most of unwanted media coverage to help turn a negative situation around.

As a leader, you need to know how to face the media and make the most of each interaction before you have to face the media. I am going to share with you some tools and strategies you can use. As your leadership role and your business grows, I also advise you to invest in media training from a credible trainer with a background in the media industry.

"It's essential to distinguish between events that are really beyond your control and events you caused yourself."
—Barbara Sher, American author and businesswoman

What Is Media Training?

Media training is a combination of things. Here is how I summarize it. With media training, you learn how to handle the pressure of being interviewed by a reporter while getting your message out and staying on point during an interview. Here are three things you should ask and answer during your media training:

1. What is my message?

2. How do I develop my message?

3. What rights do I have if the media gets the story wrong?

Your message will depend on what the situation is. For example, if you work for a company that makes widgets, and your product is being recalled for allegedly causing severe injury or death, the one thing you want to do is assure consumers your product is safe.

You develop your message by accentuating what is positive, not repeating the negative. At a news conference, a reporter may ask, "Are your customers *putting their lives at risk* by using your widgets?"

You do not want to repeat the negative by answering, "No one is *risking their lives* to use our widgets."

Instead, your message might be, "We stand behind the quality of our products and offer a money-back guarantee on all our widgets."

This answer shows the consumer you are confident in your widgets, and you are looking out for the best interest of your customers if they are not satisfied. This is an example of a win/win statement. Note, you do not repeat the negative implication that people's lives are at risk.

Develop your message by taking a reasonable, but not excessive, amount of time to gather a critical team of leaders in your company or business to process the situation. If you take too long to address the media, it tends to make the audience think you have something to hide. I always advise my clients to keep their message simple and to the point. You want to be able to deliver your message in fifteen seconds or less.

The media will not put a spin on your story how you want or think they should. Sometimes, the media may not get the facts straight. You do have rights if the facts in a story are wrong, or if you are misquoted. Ask for a retraction of the story or for the story to be corrected. Keep in mind, once information is in front of the public and your customers, it is your duty to contact the news outlet that "got it wrong" and ask them to report the correct information.

Remember, your business and reputation are at stake, and you want to take every opportunity to turn negative media attention into something positive.

Position Yourself for Positive Media Coverage

Not every media event is a crisis. Whether your company or business is new, up-and-coming or established, take every opportunity to position yourself as an expert for the media. When you turn on news stations, notice the number of experts or analysts the media relies on to help clarify or give insight into issues or problems.

Think about what expertise you offer. Are you an attorney who specializes in sports and entertainment law? Are you an accountant who understands complex tax issues, audits and financial statements? Perhaps you are a stockbroker who can explain the complexities of Wall Street. Are you a computer expert who watches trends in technology? No matter what your occupation, there is a news story that can best be explained by someone with *your* knowledge, background and credibility in that area. That someone could be *you*.

What expertise and credentials do you have that a reporter might need for a story? What is happening in your local area that you could comment on? Where could you contribute a quote or sound bite a reporter could use in an article or media interview?

As a news anchor and reporter, I kept a Rolodex® of business cards from professionals whom I met and those whom I interviewed. I often called on some of them to help add insights or provide clarity to a story. Others I worked with once and chose never to use again.

What made the difference between the ones who got airtime and those who did not? The professionals or experts who were my frequent guests were those who were available on short notice, who were articulate and knowledgeable and who had an upbeat personality.

It is easy to sit at home and say, "Hey, I can do that" when you see an interview on television. It is a very different situation when you are actually live in a television studio with lots of lights, cameras and people moving around, and you are trying to focus and answer questions in just a few seconds. There is no room for error, and you do not get the opportunity to erase what you said if you make a mistake live on the air.

How to Get Started

Now you're probably asking, "How do I become a media expert?"
The answer varies based on where you live. If you are in a small to mid-size town, you can easily contact the local newspaper, radio or television station and make them aware of your background and your business. If you have received awards and recognition in your field, be sure to highlight your accomplishments. One thing you do not want to do is pester the media or ask why they do not contact you.

If you live in a larger city, you will need to try a different approach. The media in larger markets often do not take time to vet unsolicited professionals. Instead, the media will tend to gravitate towards professionals who have been involved in a high profile event or successful company. Think of attorneys such as Gloria Allred or

Marcia Clark, who was one of the prosecutors in the O.J. Simpson trial. These attorneys have been connected to high-profile cases that involved celebrities or business tycoons. They are often called on to give their views on court cases similar to those they have been involved in.

If you live in a larger city, you can send a three- to five-minute video of yourself speaking at a conference or in a training session along with your credentials to a reporter who covers a "beat" in your area of expertise. If you are a financial planner, contact the local business editor. If you are a caterer or chef, contact the food editor. You can also send to the media any press clippings from a business periodical, college alumni magazine or other professional trade publication that spotlighted you or your company.

If you are contacted to be a media expert, be sure to make a good impression and offer to be available should the media need you to comment in the future.

Prepare for the Media

All media are not the same. Below are some basic rules to remember if you are asked to do an interview.

Television. Television interviews are often live as a story is happening. Remember, television reporters operate on tight deadlines. If you are called by a reporter to be interviewed for a story that will air later that day or that will be live in a news segment, you do not always have the luxury of asking for time to prepare.

Television is a visual medium. The audience responds first to what they see, so it is crucial for you to be well groomed, well dressed and relaxed when you are on television. This is more important for women leaders whose appearance tends to be judged more harshly than male leaders, unfortunately.

Keep in mind that too much makeup, too much hair, too much jewelry and too plunging a neckline will cause the audience to focus more on your look and not on what you are saying. The audience is distracted or distrustful when you do not look your best or if you sound or appear tense, nervous or scared.

Radio. The atmosphere for radio is slightly different from television. With a radio interview, it is important to speak well, speak clearly and slowly and know your subject matter. Do not use "crutch words" excessively, such as "well," "umm," "uh," "so," "like" and "you know." These filler words might convey to the audience that you feel uncomfortable or worse, that you are stalling because you are searching for an answer. Crutch words make you sound less confident and unsure of what you are saying.

Print. When your interview appears in the newspaper, a magazine or on the Internet, the audience cannot see or hear you. It is vital to avoid rambling or giving an incomplete answer to a reporter. The reporter is taking notes or may be recording you in order to capture your exact quotes. As much as a reporter may want to fill in the missing pieces of your incomplete answer, this is unethical and journalistically unsound. You most likely will not have a chance to review the piece before it is seen in print, so be precise and avoid ambiguous statements that can be misunderstood by the reporter.

Take Advantage of Good Media Exposure

How people perceive you or your business can either be enhanced or destroyed based on your performance in the media. Your goal is always to make the audience want to:

- Hear you

- Listen to you

- Read you

- Understand you

- Remember you

The best benefit of all positive media exposure is this: Once you position yourself to be a "go-to" expert in the media, it can translate into more business for you and your company. Those few minutes on television or radio or in print are free advertising, and who doesn't want that?

Back to the Utah mine disaster I wrote about earlier. The meltdown in the media for the Murray CEO translated into a shutdown for the mine. Livelihoods—and lives—were lost. There was little to no ability to turn around this business and media disaster. On the other hand, Debbi Fields took action in a crisis to save the reputation of her business. Today, it continues to thrive and expand.

"I've learned that people will forget what you said, people will forget what you did, but people will never forget how you made them feel."
—Maya Angelou, American poet laureate and author

Whether your company faces a crisis, or you want to position yourself as a media expert, getting media training is invaluable. How people perceive you or your business can be enhanced or destroyed based on your performance in the media. As the saying goes, "You never get a second chance to make a first impression," so get the training you need to be the best you can be. The world is watching!

MALENA CUNNINGHAM
Strategic Media Relations, Inc.

Helping you navigate media issues and public speaking

(205) 746-9942
mcunningham@
strategicmediarelationsinc.com
www.strategicmediarelationsinc.com

As founder of Strategic Media Relations, Inc., Malena brings 23 years of experience as an Emmy® award-winning television journalist to her business. She specializes in media training for company CEOs, executives and spokespeople and shows her clients how to sharpen their interviewing techniques and public speaking skills. Malena also works on video projects that help companies and agencies communicate who they are.

A strong storyteller, Malena recognizes that you and your ideas can easily be overlooked if you cannot effectively communicate them. In addition to her Emmy awards for reporting, she won the Edward R. Murrow Award and the National Association of Black Journalists Award for a half-hour documentary on the forty-year anniversary of the infamous bombing of the 16th Street Baptist Church in Birmingham, Alabama.

A sought-after speaker, trainer, emcee and consultant, Malena has successfully transitioned from the high-energy world of nightly television news to helping others navigate the media maze. She is a member of the Birmingham Association of Black Journalists and the National Association of Black Journalists and has received numerous honors for her volunteer work.

Women Leading Change

By Karen Wilhelm Buckley with Fay Freed

Are you involved in a major change these days?

Do you envision something more for your company, personal health, relationships and community?

Do you feel a compelling urge or a deep yearning to create change in your life, love or leadership, yet you lack confidence or a roadmap?

If so, it is time to get savvy about how to lead change.

Your wisdom, that clear, insightful knowing deep inside your feminine nature, understands the route into and through invigorating, yet messy, change. The transition passage, like a birth, involves intense pressure and tumultuous sensations and feelings. Acceptance, courage and love can help you give birth to a new more fulfilling future. This material can be your guide.

A Call to Women

The state of world affairs, from global warming to poverty and violence, provides plenty of left-brain, rational reasons to lead the world in new directions. What ignites the courage to act? In our experience, when an urgent inner desire coalesces, many women feel personally powerful enough to bring about small and large changes in their relationships, communities, businesses and the world.

Are you called to lead change? Around the world, women are gathering, responding to an inner urge or call to recognize, access, and promote women's leadership. In 2010, 50,000 women joined the Feminine Power® conference calls and 20,000 women signed up for The Women's Conference® in San Diego in the first days of registration. We founded The Wisdom Connection in 2009 to respond to a call from women who wanted to grow in their feminine wisdom in business and leadership. Like you, these women have become leaders in their own sphere of influence as they discover their personal power, their willingness and ability to act in the areas of life that matter the most to them.

With hearts open, women can bring new perspectives on how to get things done and what needs to be done to create a sane and sustainable world for our children and our children's children.

As coaches to women and consultants to businesses, we speak with women every day. If you are like them you might be sick and tired of self-doubt, dissatisfied with playing it safe. You are excited about new possibilities and ready to trust your own vision. You are geared up to step out and risk change.

"All serious daring starts from within."
—Eudora Welty, American writer

The Three D's for Leading Change

The positive side of change is fantastic, especially if you know the Three D's for leading change. With these tools, you can guide a change that works, has staying power and takes you where you want to go. As a woman, your tending, nurturing, catalyzing approach to change encourages collaboration, bringing change to life. Your emotional intelligence wisely guides the ups and downs.

It takes web-like awareness to understand how a change ripples out to affect others. You know that anyone can offer a "good idea" for change, but real change does not happen until the whole system, or web of relationships, agrees to change.

You understand that change unfolds in dynamic, nonlinear, non-rational and intuitive ways and that any system needs to build readiness before a change can take hold. This framework of the Three D's—Developmental Stages, Degrees, and Dimensions—makes the most of your natural leadership strengths.

We know the Three D's work! Leaders in multi-national corporations, small firms and partnerships use them to anticipate the emotional, dynamic and irregular progression of change. They come with powerful tips you can immediately apply in business and in life.

Change Is a Journey

Whether you are planning change that involves an entire corporation or just your closet, there is a transition from the present state to an altered future state. During this transition, the way you have always done things can be profoundly challenged or superficially rearranged. It is a journey. Things develop, grow, expand, arise, fall apart and work out as you go through the seven common stages of the transition passage.

The First D: Developmental Journey

The following seven stages are part of all transition passages. The path is not linear or direct. It requires you to take the unfolding, lively nature of change into account.

Developmental Stages of Change

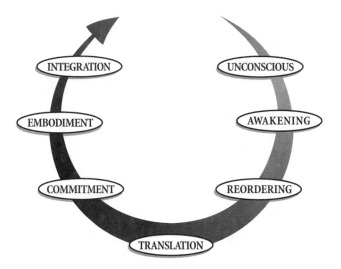

This model works for any change. As an example for this chapter, let's say you want to add online sales to your in-person storefront sales strategy. You might feel the need for change or sense it for some time before you are ready to act. Perhaps foot traffic is slowly decreasing, and a friend just made a bundle by launching an online arm to her business. Here are three tips to use as you move through the seven stages of the first D:

- **Who is where?** Notice where you are and where others are in each stage. Some people will be impatient, ready to start while others will be saying, "What change are you talking about? Why didn't you tell me earlier?" even though you might have been talking about it for weeks. Do what it takes to get everyone on the same page—both the early adoptors, those people who are quick to understand the need to change, and those people who move slowly or resist change.

- **Welcome chaos.** Chaos is a good thing. Discomfort, upset, disorder and pandemonium are often part of the transition to real and lasting change.

• **Where is the commitment?** Be proactive. Set up additional conversations with key people to anticipate problems or review the ROI—the analysis of the return on investment of your time and resources. Build sufficient commitment before implementing tangible changes.

Let's examine these stages in detail.

Stage One: Unconsciousness. This first stage is a valuable prelude when the need for change is not yet apparent. You catch hints of a possible need for change, but you are not ready to make a change, and so the hints recede. This under-the-surface time matures your internal readiness, getting you ready to accept the need for change.

You can use this time to do research, take a class or catch up on your financials as you build your willingness and ability to change. For example, you might begin to involve others in your preliminary musings about developing an online store.

Stage Two: Awakening. When you are ready to proceed with change, this stage can be dramatic and difficult or effortless. It all depends on the ratio of rigidity and fear to resilience and excitement for the new opportunity.

Smart leaders talk about the change *before* taking action. At this stage, get creative! Employ several strategies to develop widespread agreement that change is necessary and wanted. Bring inspiring online entrepreneurs into your company meeting, hold a contest for an example of the most fun fan page, bring information technology and marketing together for innovative conversations. As a savvy leader, it is up to you to set the conditions for others to wake up to the need for change.

Stage Three: Reordering. After your key people accept the need to change, the reordering stage begins. You need to dismantle parts of the old structure before building the new. To become an online company, work culture, systems, client relationships and personal time might need to be assessed. Do they need reorganization?

During reordering, the transition passage includes chaos, random disconnected ideas and questions. It is not time to implement changes. First, old ideas need to be destroyed and new ideas need to be welcomed. Reordering involves everyone in answering questions:

• What needs to change to incorporate an online strategy?

• What can remain the same?

• Who needs to change?

• In what way do I need to change?

By considering these questions, the implications of change become apparent. For many, this may be the scariest time. For others, it is the most exciting. Either way, the possibilities are endless. The usual ways of doing things are in flux. Fixed assumptions are challenged. Relationships may alter, some jobs may be eliminated, and others may need to be filled. The balance of power shifts, and innovators are valued.

Because the depth of the reordering equals the depth and breadth of the ultimate change, your role is to provide a safe environment for the chaotic questioning. Hold meetings to inquire, discover and think outside the box. Demonstrate your willingness to alter your standard patterns of behavior. Prove your ability to stretch in unprecedented ways.

Stage Four: Translation. A coherent vision begins to form out of the uncertainty of reordering, and you move into the translation stage.

Things start to come together. Articulating new intentions, a vision, a long-range plan or short-term action steps provides a real sense of momentum.

Now you start to talk coherently about real opportunities. The disconnected pieces start to fit, and your team can finally develop the capacity and plans for a full conversion to an online business.

Watch out! Even though you have talked about the impending change repeatedly, some people are just becoming aware of the need for change. Expect some resistance. Your new compelling vision might provoke an "I will not!" response.

Everyone responds differently to the need for change. Some love change. Others are slow to accept it. Even intelligent, loyal employees may not understand that the change is real until the plan is in place, and you are actively speaking about the specific, needed and imminent changes. Give people another chance to engage in their own reordering process, so they can move with you.

Stage Five: Commitment. When you get to this stage, you have reached a threshold. You have made the plans and done the research. You are at the pivotal commitment stage. Until this point, actual change has been only a possibility. Now it is real. You know when you have reached a personal or collective commitment to change a project or relationship because everything comes together. Maximize this moment and get moving!

Stage Six: Embodiment. This is the period of implementing the specific changes you outlined in the translation stage. You allocate resources, timeline key priorities and agree to milestones. Plan for a fully embodied change by identifying necessary changes to be made in the dimensions of structure (new customer relations system), behavior (IT and marketing working together in a whole new way) and consciousness (thinking virtually).

Stage Seven: Integration. This is the final stage in the transition passage. The full potential of change is experienced. New systems work in your virtual office, people settle into new routines, and inventive strategies "go viral." Integration normalizes the change and allows you to take advantage of opportunities to grow in new ways.

The Second D: Degrees of Change

These two tools can help when you are moving through the second D:

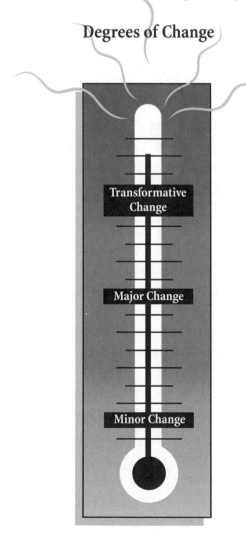

Degrees of Change

Transformative Change

Major Change

Minor Change

• **Check the temperature of the change you want.** Is it fairly cool with little impact or super hot, so that everything needs to change? Think through the extent of the expected impact before you communicate about the impending change. If the addition of an online business model is a major change, and you proceed as if it were a minor change, you can expect backlash.

• **The bigger the change, plan for more inclusion.** Stretch your thinking. Who will be affected by or is essential to this change? Who wants to keep things the way they are? Is it your spouse, boss, coworkers, another department or project manager, customers or suppliers? If you are missing buy-in, notice whom you forgot to include.

Depending on the degree of change you desire, anticipate or are experiencing, deeper levels of change mean more tumult and wider ripples of impact. It is good to plan accordingly.

A minor change is a superficial change. Maybe you test a Facebook® fan page in addition to your in-person business. This is a minor change. Almost everything stays stable, and only a few people are involved.

A major change, such as setting up a separate online store, increases the possibility for ambiguity, turmoil and chaos. It involves a search for underlying causes and a significant reorganization in systems, habitual work styles and personnel. By its nature, it is more systemic. The impact of a major change extends further than a minor change and may affect all parts of the business or community.

A transformative change is rare and is to be taken very seriously. This degree of change contains a fundamental shift in consciousness, values or perceptions. It is like learning to swim. It is hard to imagine until you finally float and then hard to forget because you made a basic change in how you view water. An inspiring vision, the death of a loved one or a health surprise might catalyze a transformative level change.

"A leader is anyone willing to help, anyone who sees something that needs to change and takes the first steps to influence that situation. . . Everywhere in the world, no matter the economic or social circumstances, people step forward to try and make a small difference. . . And this is why we need to step forward for what we care about."
—Margaret Wheatley, American founder, Berkana Institute

The Third D: Dimensions of Change

A change is incomplete without shifts in the three dimensions of behavior, structure and consciousness. These shifts involve both people and the organization. When any one of the three is missing, the system easily reverts to old ways of doing things. Here are two tools to help you in the third D:

- **Change your thinking.** Discover your restrictive thoughts. Are your old beliefs maintaining the status quo even though you want a change? Repeating, "I am too old to shift to a virtual world" shuts your mind down. You may need to change your thinking in order to increase your capacity for change.

- **Design the conditions for your success.** Look at your business structures. Which ones support old behaviors and ways of thinking? Which ones support change? For instance, if your assistant resists the change in his role, clearly communicate your new expectations.

Let's look at these three dimensions of change.

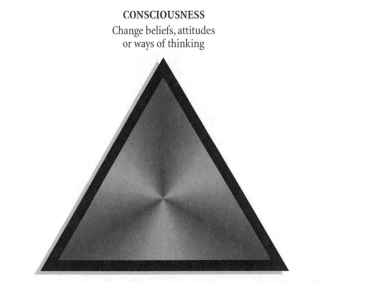

CONSCIOUSNESS
Change beliefs, attitudes
or ways of thinking

STRUCTURE
Change the systems and processes
to match the intended change

BEHAVIOR
Change ways of acting
to match the intended change

Behavior. Ranging from completing the simplest everyday tasks to handling a crisis, behaviors need to change to align with the intended change. In an online business, you might change daily behavior to tweet, post on Facebook or respond to customer questions via email.

Structure. Changes are curtailed unless you reorganize the agreements that dictate how you relate to each other and the systems that direct the flow of daily work. Systems or procedures, such as budgeting, interoffice communications, time management and physical layout, are structures that may need to change.

Consciousness. Deep-seated beliefs and old-time attitudes, ideology or norms that shape your actions and the organization's culture must change to lead, match and support behavior and structural changes.

"These are the times when we stand humbly and boldly in the presence of our own great promise. These are the days when through our decisions and actions, we determine our legacy for those to come."
—Jean Houston, PhD, American visionary and scholar

The 3 D's will give you more understanding of how to lead change and get where you want to go. Be bold and confident as you step out and wisely guide others through the transition passages of change. We invite you to be the wise feminine leader you already are and respond to the compelling urge of that yearning or call inside you that will not be denied.

Change is scary, exhilarating and necessary. It is the only way to create the business and life you most want and to contribute the full potential of your leadership to the world.

Leading change that works in our families, communities and organizations, and becoming change agents in the world is a journey. Resolve to develop savvy leadership and the ability to guide inspiring and effective changes for all concerned.

KAREN WILHELM BUCKLEY
Director, The Wisdom Connection
(415) 888-3099
info@thewisdomconnection.com
www.thewisdomconnection.com

FAY FREED
Co-Founder, Star Consulting
(415) 897-0689
fay@starconsulting.org
www.starconsulting.org

Karen and Fay have long been recognized together and separately for their programs and coaching that engender more effective leadership and strengthen a woman's natural authority through powerful, wise, feminine methodologies. They have worked with corporate, government and nonprofit organizations as consultants and leadership coaches.

As Director of The Wisdom Connection, Karen Buckley coaches and consults with women and women-owned businesses ready to move to the next level of leadership by developing feminine wisdom and power. She is a published author and international speaker on organizational change and the invisible sides of leadership. Since 1991, Karen has been the principal of Communicore, a consulting firm that develops wise leadership and effective teams in business.

In 1994, Fay co-founded The Center for Women's Leadership, whose purpose was to empower women to realize their personal power and to manifest their most heartfelt visions. Over the course of seven years, hundreds of women from all walks of life across the United States participated in the programs offered by the Center. Now, through Star Consulting, Fay offers consulting services and programs to empower women, men, and couples who are making new lifestyle choices.

Lead Change and Empower Success

By Jan McDonough, WABC

What is change? Change is something different from what currently exists. It is becoming different or altered.

Change is a powerful word.

Change allows transformation to occur.

Change conjures a multitude of emotions—some positive, many negative. How you choose to handle change is the key to being able to lead and empower through change successfully.

> *"If you change the way you look at things,*
> *the things you look at change."*
> —Wayne Dyer, American speaker and author

Why change? Change is necessary. It is a required component of progress, and it offers you opportunities for growth, new knowledge and abundance.

Change is constant. It is the one thing you can count on consistently throughout life. In fact, *change is life*, and it can strike fear in the hearts of many. Most of this is fear of the unknown.

When confronted with change, you can find yourself stuck in a tornado of questions and doubts:

• What will it be like when the change actually occurs?

• Will I know what to do?

• Will I be able to work with it?

• Will it hold me back from getting where I want to go?

Remember, change is the only real constant in life. It has propelled us forward as a society.

Change is *good!* Change takes you from your comfort zone. You think and act differently during and following change. It has allowed us, as a society and as individuals to break through barriers; to see things in color, not just black and white; and to travel the world—and even to the moon.

Lives change dramatically when a new baby arrives or you receive a promotion. These are positive changes. They are good things, yet even positive change requires a great deal of adjustment.

> *"Something which we think is impossible now is not impossible in another decade."*
> —Constance Baker Motley, first African-American federal judge

You face many changes every day. Some are simple adjustments or tune-ups to your normal routine, or they are just preparation for the next step. Sometimes, only a small tweak takes place. Sometimes, change is more like an overhaul. Whatever the case may be, a change of some sort occurs daily.

With more than twenty years of experience in direct sales and fifty years of living, I have become known as a "change agent." As silly and as hard to believe as this is, I actually *love* change! I seek out change—big ones, small ones, macro changes and little, bitty micro ones.

In this chapter, I will share some tips to help you lead and empower yourself and others while in the midst of those bigger, scarier, "monsters-under-the-bed" sorts of changes. I have discovered these time-tested techniques along my journey of thriving during change.

Here are four steps that will allow you to shift your view of change and truly believe that change is *good*.

Step One: Investigate

Gather all available information that relates to the change you are facing. Think about the timing of the change and answer these questions:

• Is this an immediate change?

• Is this change occurring on a specific date?

• Will this change occur gradually, giving me time to adjust as it happens?

• Will I need to relocate or change jobs?

• How will the change affect my family?

For example, if you or your spouse are facing a potential promotion that requires relocation, some of the areas you need to investigate are schools, housing, transferring things like medical insurance and primary care providers, job opportunities for other family members and so on.

By investigating, you will gain clarity around this change. Knowledge is power that gives you the information you need to move forward and make the decisions change often requires.

Step Two: Evaluate

Make a list of all the pros and cons related to this change. This process helps you further alleviate any confusion that has been building. Give yourself all the time you can to thoroughly evaluate the good, the bad and even the ugly aspects of the change you are facing. You will discover options during this process. Carefully list them as they come into your thought process. Using our example, here are some things to evaluate:

• How could this affect me? My family?

• What do I really know about this change?

• Could this be the right time and the right place for this change?

• What will be the best way to prepare the family for this transition?

• How are environmental responsibilities handled in this new area?

• What types of events are offered within this community and surrounding areas?

You will notice I used the word "could." This is where your attitude comes into play. How you react to change is all on you. It is a choice.

Choose to view change as an opportunity and embrace it. Fear and excitement feel the same in your body! It is only in your mind that you label what you are feeling as either fear or excitement. Develop the mental muscle of positivity by reminding yourself daily that change is really and truly a good—no, a *great*—thing.

"I am convinced that life is 10 percent what happens to me and 90 percent how I react to it."
—Charles Swindoll, American minister

After you complete the evaluation step, break the transition down into goals.

• What needs to happen short term?

• Is this truly the future I am looking for?

• Is it just a stepping-stone along the way to something else?

• Where do I see myself and my family in one year, five years, ten years from now?

Step Three: Educate

Develop strategies to help you share about the change with those who need the information. Work diligently to ensure the strategies are in a format that gets your message across without creating additional anxiety for those who will be working through this change. Develop a timeline of when to best share certain pieces of information strategically throughout the change process with the intent to provide clarity, instill confidence and foster a willingness to collaborate even during the most stressful of changes.

This is especially important for changes in the workplace. Sharing everything all at once with those you are leading in an effort to be transparent and open can backfire during high-tension changes. Take time to analyze the behavior styles and coping skills of those involved and share just enough information to put them at ease as much as possible.

Remember, some people have behavioral styles that thrive in change—like me!—while others need more time and have questions they need answered. Some things to consider to help you determine the change style of those involved are:

- Do they need the basics of the change laid out ahead of time? How can you best do this to minimize negative responses?

- Do they need time to process? If so, how much time?

- Do I have the necessary time to offer them right now? If not, what can I do?

- Will they be excited and greatly anticipate the change as a new challenge or will they resist it and be afraid? How will I handle each reaction? What will I say?

- Will they feel the need to fight the change? How will I deal with this response?

- What assistance can I offer them to help them cope with the change?

Some people will need more information before they can begin to accept the change. Some are naturally resistant to change of any kind. Remind yourself and them that the world as we know it today would not exist if it were not for change. The advantage is learning how to deal with change and allowing it to lead to success.

Step Four: Identify the Impact

Take time to identify and address the effects of this change on yourself and those involved in the change. When change becomes inevitable, complaining becomes wasted energy. Instead of complaining, take that energy and channel it toward improving the situation.

- How much of this change is beyond my control?

- How much of this change am I, and those I lead, being forced to accept?

- What is important for each person involved?

- How will this change affect the environment?

- What fears will people have around this change?

Many people experience fear and anxiety around how a specific change may affect them, their family and/or their businesses. Leading and empowering through change is fear management. I like to think of it as *fear-busting*! Ask others these questions:

- What is your biggest concern about making this move?

- How can I help you?

- Do you realize what this move can do for your future?

- Can you start to feel the excitement and how it is dissolving your concerns?

When the change is your idea, you can more easily embrace it. If the change is not your idea, there can be great resistance on your part. The same is true of others. It is easier for people to embrace change when it is their idea, and more challenging when they are not the source of the change.

People tend to become complacent with their routines. They have been working with things just fine as they are and feel no need to change. They are comfortable with their lives and jobs and want the status quo to remain. Change disrupts the status quo, and the adjustment can add a great deal of stress to your life and the lives of those affected by it. However, by learning to accept change as a needed constant, by identifying the fear and removing it, you can begin to open your heart and mind to embrace it, resulting in the fear and stress just melting away.

"When one door of happiness closes, another opens; but often we look so long at the closed door that we do not see the one which has been opened for us."
—Helen Keller, American author, political activist and lecturer

Step Five: Lead by Example

A leader must be open to change, and effective leadership requires the leader to change first. Once you have embraced and developed the skills for navigating change, you must continue to use those skills to support others through change. You must always be receptive to new ideas and the good change may bring. Great leaders not only talk about what should be done, they do it! As the leader, you will discover your excitement generates energy for yourself and others. The more you embrace change, the more you become an instrument of change in the lives of others. For more on this subject, see "Leadership Is a Growth Process" by LaNell Silverstein on page 45.

Leading through change means you must develop trust with the people involved. The more people trust you, the more they will follow your direction. Trust is an emotional attachment that binds people together. The leader's ability to trust and be trusted can mean the success or failure of the change for all involved. When you are committed to a change, you will realize greater acceptance from those you are leading. You set the example that allows others to become supportive and more eager to work toward the common goal. You also need to provide examples of other changes that have been made that have produced positive results.

"True originality consists not in a new manner but in a new vision."
—Edith Wharton, American author

As you lead others through a change or series of changes, keep them apprised about how things are moving along and review what may be needed in the way of an adjustment. Acknowledge positive results as you go through the phases of change and communicate your progress as you and your team transform. Using our example of the family move, here are some things you could say to encourage your family members and acknowledge their efforts:

• *We only have seven more boxes to put away and the kitchen will be unpacked and ready for cooking.*

• *You have done a great job in setting up your bedroom.*

• *I am glad you are excited about your new school and your new friends.*

• *This community has so much to offer us.*

Leading Change Requires Vision and Faith

Allow yourself the opportunity to paint the picture by creating a vision of the result. This vision will become a positive driver as you bring others on board with the change. Keep the vision in front of everyone as each adjusts to the change and works through it. Everyone loves to see the sun at the end of the storm. This is what you are creating with this vision of the result. The sun will shine again!

When I find myself in the midst of one of those "monster-under-the-bed" changes, I consistently return to the *Serenity Prayer:* "God, grant me the serenity to accept the things I cannot change, the courage to change the things I can, and the wisdom to know the difference."

Theologian Dr. Reinhold Niebuhr conceived the original *Serenity Prayer* in a little stone cottage in Heath, Massachusetts. However, the first form of this prayer originated with Boethius, a Roman philosopher. This little prayer can make a huge impact on your decisions. The *Serenity Prayer* has the power to help define some of the changes you do not understand when they are happening. Think about it.

When you take the time to consider the main elements of change, you will find the internal power to accept and work with the adjustments required by it. Empowerment, positive energy and excitement are just a few of your possible outcomes. When you give change a chance, greatness can be discovered.

As you look at your past in comparison to where you are today, you would not have come this far if not for change. You have gone from childishness to maturity, from a lack of understanding to savvy leadership.

I challenge you to embrace change with excitement and enthusiasm. Use the tools in this chapter to help you in the process of leading through change, empowering your own success while helping others achieve theirs.

Change does not necessarily create a win or lose situation. It is how you play the game of adjusting to change that matters. Simply by taking the time to *investigate, evaluate, educate, identify* and *lead by example,* you have created some valuable tools to help you embrace and lead change successfully. For more on the subject of leading change, See "Women Leading Change" by Karen Wilhelm Buckley with Fay Freed on page 155 and Carole Sacino's chapter "Leadership Is in the Palm of Your Hand" on page 179.

JAN MCDONOUGH, WABC
Tupperware® Elite Executive Director
Founder, Attitude Adventures

*Exploring the Unlimited
Path of Possibilities!*

(763) 971-8583
jan@attitudeadventures.com
www.attitudeadventures.com

For more than twenty years, Jan McDonough has worked with individuals and organizations to make a difference in the lives of others. She supports both men and woman from all walks of life, including stay-at-home parents, career changers and established professionals. Creating and executing action plans is her unique way of empowering people to realize their potential and achieve a higher quality of life. She gives them success tools, builds their self-confidence and guides them on the path to making their dreams come true.

Currently based in Minneapolis, Minnesota, Jan has earned many top honors from her direct sales company in the United States, North America and worldwide and from the Direct Selling Women's Alliance® She is certified as a Dream Coach® and as a Group Dream Coach® through Dream Coach University® in California. Her most recent accomplishment is certification through both the World Association of Business Coaches® and through the DSWA Coach Excellence Program®

When Jan speaks to audiences in the United States and abroad, she reaches out and connects with everyone by keeping her speeches and trainings fun, informative, interactive and inspiring.

Leadership Is in the Palm of Your Hand

By Carole Sacino

When I was seven, I had open-heart surgery that compromised the quality of my voice. For many years, I had little to no voice at all, and the voice I did have was soft and raspy. I could not project it. Everything in my life revolved around my lack of voice.

In 2010, I discovered I had a paralyzed vocal cord and had surgery to correct the problem. I now have a voice, but all those years of being voiceless taught me how to be a master of self-expression without having a voice.

Leadership Is Like a Palm Tree

The palm tree is resilient. It is one of the few trees not blown down or uprooted in stormy weather. The palm bends and does not break. It can touch the ground with its top branches, and when the wind dies down, it bounces back, its root system stronger than ever.

On the other hand, all kinds of other trees are blown down and uprooted in storms. Even the mighty oak with its relatively shallow roots is no match for 100-mile-per-hour winds. To be a savvy leader, you need to be like a palm tree. You need flexibility to work in the eye of the storm and stay standing at the end. Like the palm, you may bend, but you do not break. You can weather the storms because you know they are temporary, and you recognize them as opportunities to grow and expand your personal power, passion and purpose in work and life.

Like many women of my generation, I spent many years in the corporate environment, fighting my way up the ranks in predominately male workplaces. Being in sales gave me personal control over my career path because bottom line results were the measurement of success. My role models were the men I worked for or competed against, and they drove my behavior. Despite my success, I was not moving in the direction that gave me personal power, passion and purpose.

> *"Limitations live only in the minds, but if we use our imagination, our possibilities become limitless."*
> —Jamie Paolinetti, American professional cyclist

Finally, in 2006, I made the bold move of leaving the corporate environment. My purpose is consulting, coaching, mentoring, training and development, and cultivating women business leaders so they can tap into their personal power, passion and purpose. My passion is to help others discover their voice, create choices about work and life and get results from the inside out. I want to share my understanding with you, so you can enhance your leadership skills and become a voice for women.

Early in my career, I learned a set of principles that still serve me today. I call them my PALM Principles. There are three sets, and I hope you find them as useful as I do.

PALM Principles #1

Proactively demonstrate how your company can leverage your talents to achieve bottom line results.

Address challenges and overcome obstacles.

Leverage your drive, knowledge and relationships to achieve measurable results.

Maximize opportunities to learn and grow professionally and be successful.

Ironically, my first sales position was with a leading dictation company, and it was a straight commission role. It was a tremendous experience to break out of my comfort zone, bend and not break, and build resilience. I put together a strategy:

- Listen to the market and ask what problem I can help solve.

- Learn about the market, the competition and the technology, creating a unique selling proposition.

- Lead with questions and curiosity to discover what the market wants and needs.

- Leverage what they need with what you can provide.

I knew this was a working strategy back in 1978 after I called on a computer technology distributor and met with the vice president of sales. We were discussing how he could help his sales team be more effective and efficient using dictation equipment when he asked the president to come in and hear my pitch. After listening with great interest, I was offered a job at this company. Intrigued, honored, surprised and excited, I said, "Yes, after you buy this dictation solution!" They bought a smaller version of what I was selling, and I got a salaried sales position from them. I was the first female sales person in the company, and my role was supporting sales representatives, some of whom were not as good as I was at sales.

Situations like this provide an amazing opportunity to put the power of *intention* into play. Visualize the outcome you want to achieve and put all your attention and actions toward that outcome. I became focused on success and recognition—on proving a woman could succeed in sales and move onto the next big opportunity! However, something had to change quickly if I was to make my mark.

I was working with what we called the "Old Boy's Club." All business opportunities happened on the golf course or at the men's club where the "boys" shared drinks and business leads and women were excluded. Putting the PALM Principles into action, I decided to go where the deals were made. I learned how to swing a golf club. I was not a great golfer, but I was good enough to feel somewhat confident on the course.

At work and on the course, I placed myself in situations where I could suggest creative ideas to management. My ideas were unique game changers and helped differentiate me from my competition. Management listened and implemented many of my ideas—and I was not given credit!

During this era, women were often not valued or validated in organizations, and their voices were not heard. *My voice was not heard.* My number one need is to be heard and since our needs drive our behavior, this was a catalyst for me to thrive in the face of adversity. I dug in, gained knowledge of the business and built valuable relationships. I moved up in the organization and eventually made it to the executive suite—a place with very few women.

When the CEO wanted a high-level golf event with key client executives, I was asked to chair this event because I had the connections, I could multi-task and get things done and I am a woman. Therefore, I would not mind organizing it. Not one man offered to take this on, so I agreed to do it.

> *"The difference between possible and impossible lies in the person's determination."*
> —Tommy Lasorda, America Major League Baseball® player and manager

I managed the entire event and even established a foursome of women—the only women who would be present. At the last minute, however, they cancelled because they were intimidated with the all-male line-up. That made me the only woman present.

Tee-time came, and I approached three friendly male customers who were happy to ride with me. They asked me to lead the group, and I agreed although I had no clue what I was doing and had never driven a golf cart. After a few false starts, I got us to the first hole. It was time to step up and hit the ball. All those male eyes watched me. I stifled my nerves, prayed I would at least connect with the ball, gathered my courage and swung! I hit it very nicely over the green a good distance to the hole. I breathed a sigh of relief, graciously accepted the praise of my foursome, and the rest of the day was easier and more enjoyable.

Where can you apply PALM Principles #1 in your work?

• Does your company know the value you bring to their bottom line results? If not, how can you demonstrate this?

• Do you take on challenges and overcome obstacles?

• How can you leverage your drive, knowledge and relationships to achieve measureable results?

• What opportunities do you have to learn and grow professionally and be successful?

More women entered the business and became powerful change leaders. My passion was to discover and cultivate strong women business leaders and hire and recommend them for available positions in my company and in the market.

"Awareness precedes action."
—Ellie Drake, American businesswoman, speaker, doctor, founder of Braveheart Women Global Community

PALM Principles #2

Persevere with passion, purpose and possibilities.

Aspire to authenticity and openness when you inform, involve and engage the business, strategy and people.

Lead by example and keep moving forward with courage, conviction and commitment.

Mentor, motivate and create memorable moments that matter.

In 1990, I moved on to a B2B technology magazine that was in serious decline. Over six years, we went through several management changes, an organizational merger and acquisition, major competitive investments and pressure to capture and grow market share and mind share—when your customers think of you early and often. Every change in management created a change in the mission, message and position in the market. It also created confusion. Despite this, we had tremendous loyalty from our team as we fought to stay alive as a magazine.

When the CEO offered me the job of publisher, I hesitated. There were very few female publishers in the business. I still hesitated. The magazine was in a desperate decline and bold changes were needed if we were to regain market share. This job seemed like the worst possible choice, so why did I finally agree to take it?

This job was a test of leadership, and leaders have an unwavering belief in possibilities. They have the passion to see things through and the purpose to make a difference. Leaders bring the drive needed to support the dedication and determination of a team to keep going. PALM Principles #2 came into play.

As a leader, you have to persevere with passion, purpose and possibilities. Everyone will look to you for information on how to respond and act. You must be the model you want others to follow.

You need to be authentic and open. Candid, honest communication is necessary to reassure people they will be protected and cared for. You want your team and customers to have faith in your ability to lead them successfully through the change. It is important for you to clearly articulate the value proposition and drive the business to win.

I was always looking for high potential women and found a few who joined our team. Even in a state of change, they were hungry and willing to learn everything they could about sales and leadership. The opportunity to mentor and motivate them through the challenges and for them to gain great success early and often was extremely rewarding. Today, each of them is a highly successful and powerful executive business leader. This was a great example of leading change and paying it forward by mentoring!

Over the next two years, we had a remarkable turnaround in market share and mind share. However, this was not enough for the company to keep investing money, and the decision was made to sell the technology magazines. We had a serious buyer, and even though the buyer underbid the offer, the management team was considering it. I could not let that happen without a fight. It was time to show my courage, conviction and commitment to this business and to my team.

I made it clear to the management team: They would be better off leveraging their rich, robust subscriber list and launch a digital-only version of the publication that would require a minimum investment to keep it going. They considered my proposal and decided to support it.

This was a good next step for the company, but not for me. After eight long challenging and fulfilling years, it was time to take all that I had learned and apply it elsewhere.

> *"When nothing is sure - everything is possible."*
> —Margaret Drabble, English novelist

Where can you apply PALM Principles #2 in your work?

• Do you have perseverance and lead with passion, purpose and possibilities?

• Are you authentic and open when you inform, involve and engage the business, strategy and people?

• Do you lead by example and keep moving forward with courage, conviction and commitment?

• Do you mentor, motivate and create memorable moments that matter?

PALM Principles #3

Pay attention in the present moment in order to change course and shift direction as needed.

Act after understanding because you do not know what you do not know until you know it, and only then can you take action.

Listen, learn and lead with empathy, understanding and respect for others at all times.

Motivate and engage with a sense of humor.

My next opportunity to hone my leadership skills came from a company for which I previously worked, and I found myself back in my old office working for a different business unit. The opportunity was to turn up market buzz and product offerings, to shift from selling a single product to selling a suite of product offerings, creating a solution for our customers, with the goal to gain mind share and market share with key accounts across the country.

This was a great, new market strategy for external clients, but it posed a threat to our internal clients—the other business leaders and their sales teams in the organization. Our changes would take away their business opportunities, relationships and revenue. I needed to use every leadership skill and talent I had to develop a consistent approach that would inspire others and get results from the inside out!

Before leading your organization forward with major changes that impact large areas and groups of people, you must ask and answer these questions:

- What is our purpose for introducing this change? A purpose is contributing to something greater than ourselves.

- What is the unique value proposition we bring to all parties by implementing this change?

- Who is involved?

- What are the resources and talents we need to succeed?

- What are the possible obstacles that could get in the way of our success?

- What are the potential rewards and risks?

- How can we leverage our talents and build new skills for maximum results?

- How can we communicate effectively and inform, involve and engage others in a positive, proactive way?

- How can we champion the change with clarity, compassion and commitment to create win-win opportunities?

Excited to announce this unique strategy to the market, we quickly realized our strategy was too big to be effective and efficiently supported. We took a step back and redefined it. Our internal customers liked this new approach and were motivated to support it because it gave them unique and competitive opportunities and a bigger seat at the customer table.

After a rocky start to the program, we experienced many twists and turns on the road of change, and there were days when we wanted to laugh and cry. It was important to keep a sense of humor through all of this. After all we weren't doing brain surgery! We found our sweet spot and honed our strategies that created more win/win/win scenarios internally and externally. Once again, PALM Principles helped us to meet this challenge.

How can you use the PALM Principles to meet massive change head on and succeed?

• Practice paying attention and staying in the present moment in order to change course and shift direction as needed. Do not let your attention wander!

• Learn and study the situation and your alternatives before you act because you do not know what you do not know until you know it and only then, you can take action.

• Become a good listener, learn all you can about your business and leading people, so you can lead with empathy, understanding and respect for others at all times.

• Remember to motivate and engage people with a sense of humor.

• Never take yourself too seriously!

For more on leading and managing change see "Women Leading Change" by Karen Wilhelm Buckley with Fay Freed on page 155, and Jan McDonough's chapter, "Lead Change and Empower Success" on page 167.

Reach Out and Take Leadership

Palms do not break when storms batter them—they weather them! Palms are resilient and bounce right back. They bend but do not break, and every time they are bent, their root systems are strengthened by the stress and are given new opportunities for growth.

You already have what you need to be a great and savvy leader. Tap into your personal power, passion and purpose, listen to your inner voice, lead the life and do the work you choose. Storms come and go, and the wind will blow and blow. When you are knocked down, use the PALM Principles to bounce back stronger and more resilient than ever. Leadership *is* in the palm of your hand.

CAROLE SACINO
Founder, Turning Point Institute

(617) 299-1198

carole@turningpointinstitute.com

www.turningpointinstitute.com

Carole Sacino established Turning Point Institute after a successful career as a woman business leader and senior level executive. She has experience in and teaches others how to use the *power of voice and choice* to create a more powerful, passionate and purposeful contribution in work and life. Her company provides custom solutions when the goal is to engage, commit and motivate individuals and teams toward a common purpose with results from the inside out! The company motto is: *Keep it simple, effective, engaging and experiential for real change to happen.*

Carole believes you have everything you need to be the most powerful you! She helps you tap into your personal power, passion and purpose with courage, hope and confidence. She has a strong passion for mentoring, coaching, discovering and developing high potential, and cultivating successful women leaders.

Before starting Turning Point Institute, Carole spent twenty-plus years in the publishing and media industry holding sales and senior executive level leadership positions that drove business and change throughout the organization. She is a certified professional coach, master practitioner in energy leadership and emotional intelligence and a Motivation Factor® alliance partner.

Becoming an International Leader

By Lindsay Shields

Do you want to get involved in projects outside your own community?

Do you want to connect with other individuals or organizations around the globe?

Do you long to lead and support others despite the fact you have much to learn and experience yourself?

Do you enjoy being in a continual learning mode?

Are you eager to use your leadership skills to help women in other countries and from other cultures?

If you answered yes to any of these questions, international leadership offers you the opportunity to make a contribution on a large, colorful stage by interacting and working with women around the world.

Desire and drive are the strong underpinnings for any leader, especially for those in cultures where women's roles have traditionally been subordinate to men. As a leader, you must be willing to go outside your comfort zone and excel, to leave the known for the unknown and to add to your life experience. International leadership is the classroom where you can experience all of this.

"In the time of your life, live—so that in that wondrous time you shall not add to the misery and sorrow of the world, but shall smile to the infinite delight and mystery of it."
—William Saroyan, American author

I became interested in volunteerism as a child. I grew up in a two-bedroom home and shared one bedroom with two sisters. I thought it was crowded until I learned about entire families who lived in just one small room. I went abroad and saw families cooking meals outdoors on fire pits while chickens walked freely over open flour sacks. I wanted to know how people around the world lived in and survived such conditions. This desire inspired me to take my leadership skills and put them to work to help the women of the world.

Over the years, I have helped in my community by volunteering in social service organizations. When traveling to impoverished, underdeveloped countries, I noticed that successful programs for empowering others to achieve better lives were accomplished through strong, compassionate leadership.

Is there a local organization that would benefit from your leadership skills? Do you already provide voluntary leadership to that organization? If you want to move to a larger stage, start small. Use your leadership skills to benefit your local community and take that experience to benefit an international organization.

Your leadership is needed everywhere from your own backyard to the international sphere. If you have a strong, compelling desire to make a difference in the world, I will show you how to turn that desire into action.

Broaden Your Exposure to the World of Differences

In your own community, you probably feel comfortable knowing how local systems work. However, in another country or culture, the rules can be much different.

I have been to Nepal twice, and on the second trip, I was fortunate to experience volunteer leadership through two exceptional women: long-time friend Dr. Michele Andina, a nurse and doctor of anthropology, and Nepali leader Rita Thapa of Kathmandu, who started several non-governmental organizations (NGOs) to empower women. Working with them helped me focus on the challenges of helping others build a better existence.

Dr. Andina had worked for numerous international health organizations over the years and had visited women's groups around the world. She was a frequent visitor to Nepal and wanted to share her birthday with friends on a trek in the Annapurna Mountains of that country. She arranged for our group of first-time visitors to meet with women's groups in the villages where we stayed overnight.

We listened to women from geographically-challenged rural areas talk about molding leadership skills to help them better raise their families alone. While their husbands were gone for years serving in the army, they ran all aspects of their village businesses. These women were awe-inspiring. Their energetic leadership in forming business coalitions kept their villages running smoothly. Dealing with new issues day in and day out heightened their organizational and leadership skills. When the husbands retired and tended to sit around, the women would organize them to do the heavier work, such as repairing roads or building houses. These women learned leadership out of necessity and found a way to build coalitions and businesses!

Have you been placed in a leadership role out of necessity? What did you learn about leadership from this experience? What can you teach others about leadership?

"Caring can be learned by all human beings, can be worked into the design of every life, meeting an individual need as well as a pervasive need in society."
—Mary Catherine Bateson, American cultural anthropologist

Rita Thapa has founded many organizations including TEWA®— meaning "support" in Nepali. TEWA is a nonprofit NGO that provides alternative business models to promote sustainable development and women's empowerment. Its goal is to end Nepal's hierarchies of gender, class, caste, ethnicity, age and geography.

My group visited TEWA, had discussions with staff and visited women-run businesses built with TEWA support and direction. Studying Rita helped me understand the following leadership concepts:

• Leadership in underdeveloped countries is pointedly different from leadership in America. To lead in other countries and cultures, you must observe others' customs and habits, and appreciate the differences without judgment or bias.

• Leadership in poor communities demands creative thinking and creative actions on many levels.

• While meeting the basic needs of food and shelter are paramount to leaders, leadership must be both compassionate and forceful.

Because volunteering internationally brings unique challenges, it is important that you become clear about what you want from the experience.

• Why are you interested in international leadership?

• What are your local and international goals?

• Can you start a program in the United States and translate it to benefit those in need in another country?

• Are you eager to find and use creative solutions that are positive, productive and fun?

• What areas really move you and inspire you to act? Women's roles? Hunger? Childcare?

• What issues and challenges do you want to focus on?

Network in the International Community

If your goal is international leadership, start extending your range of friends and colleagues in the international arena by tapping into local and international resources that have like-interests to your goals. For example, through TEWA, Rita Thapa pioneered the idea of local, social philanthropy. She approached local sources rather than going to foreign sources for support, and this was an organizational game-changer. TEWA promotes a sense of ownership among Nepalis for their development initiatives and awards grants, not loans, to the overlooked sector of women in rural areas. This, in turn, builds stronger communities by empowering local women enterprises. Eventually these grant recipients become TEWA donors, bringing the process full-circle.

These women then become a network bonded through common goals that naturally become stronger through the good work done and the rewards gained. It was a pleasure to see women in action and to know that empowering women to build sustainability through development, education and leadership programs can ultimately change the world. We wish we could clone everyone to make the process grow faster.

When we returned from our trek, we added our support to Dr. Adina's efforts by starting the Jagriti Foundation.® "Jagriti" means "awakening" in Nepali. Dr. Andina knew the extensive work needed to support, educate and empower women. Her knowledge and empathy for women, especially in countries with caste systems, brought the needed worldview to the Jagriti Foundation, which incorporated a two-pronged approach.

Awakening Journeys guided Americans through underdeveloped countries starting in Afghanistan, India, Nepal and Pakistan, touring historical sites and meeting leaders who built local support organizations for women.

The Bridging Worlds program provided scholarships for young women who were budding leaders in their fields and who served as second-in-command in their organizations. These scholarships provided a three-month travel internship to the United States to work with an organization with a mission and goals similar to theirs. The ultimate goal was to take their new-found knowledge and tools back to their country to add to and expand their own organizations.

Not only did these young women have amazingly life-changing experiences during their time in the United States, but they also were schooled in fundraising, grant writing, outreach, public relations and business management. As assistant directors, they now had more experience to help build leadership abilities to take back to their home countries and to help expand their organization's capacities to build programs and assist others. Building programs to support women in under-developed countries is the only way to ensure positive change for a sustainable future of equality and positive growth.

Becoming involved in the Jagriti Foundation was a big step for me to take onto the international stage. You do not have to start with such a large undertaking—you can start at any level, anywhere. Many organizations need your skills—some of them are right outside your door.

If you want to start small, take on a local challenge and start your own nonprofit. For example, the founder and head of THRIVE Publishing,™ Caterina Rando, started A Good Deed Tea. Friends gather for high tea and donate money to a charitable organization. It is a simple idea, yet a meaningful one that brings charity home. Friends of mine in Long Beach started a progressive dinner in their homes once a month at the cost of a mid-priced dinner and donated the proceeds of each evening to different charities. Internationally, for only $25, you can support a variety of women's businesses through online organizations. These nonprofits use your donation to make small business loans to women-owned businesses and, when paid back, you can reinvest into another business. Not only does the giving continue, it makes you feel good to know that your dollars are at work around the world.

You can also look for a woman in your network who is interested in or has already expanded her leadership internationally. How can you collaborate on a project or help with an existing project?

"I am awed by the strength and commitment that young women leaders demonstrate. They have a strong desire to learn and grow their leadership skills and are determined to use their new tools to help women in their communities become stronger with each passing day."
—Rita Thapa, Nepalese civic leader, Founder of TEWA and past board chair, Global Fund for Women®

Learn to Lead by Stepping Aside

I have been involved in groundbreaking, leadership programs from Nepal to China, and the Jagriti experience was the most life changing.

The Jagriti Foundation process started with researching and accessing limited information in remote areas, searching for budding leaders and bringing them together in a secure, positive setting to experience the value of leadership workshops. In India, 24 organizations from around the country met for a three-day workshop to talk about the scholarships, the internships and the program goals. Many women's organizations came together for the first time. They studied and built relationships, then their peers chose the most passionate and capable leaders to become Jagriti interns. This sound and viable process also offered a forum that, when repeated, will capture those interested in leading and provide the process for growth into leadership roles.

When you interact with local people who are eager to learn about leadership and want to help their communities, you quickly discover how strong their desire is to learn, and discover their determination to incorporate new tools and to teach others a new path to success.

In another country, you must decide how you can offer assistance or drive an effort without taking over pride of ownership in the project. Your goal is to involve local organizations, mentor others and groom local leaders. Dr. Andina had the foresight, skills and tools to build a program that solicited women's organizations across four countries and hosted seminars, workshops, internships and mentorships. Then she had the wisdom to step aside and let the women she trained and mentored take the lead.

How can you provide opportunities for potential leaders to learn from you and learn from each other within a secure, supportive setting?

Here are some key tools for mentoring and growth that I have learned through my work:

• Provide appropriate stimuli for young women who would most likely be the future executive directors or the leaders of women-supportive organizations.

- Build self-confidence through examples of other women in business.

- Openly share country and cultural differences to minimize those differences. Offer positive, supportive and open opportunities for exchanging ideas and exploring new life changes.

- Expand your experiences and beliefs with others in a supportive environment.

It is surprising how little effort it takes to inspire someone who really wants to learn. Many of the women we trained in leadership returned to their countries to build stronger organizations and to extend their leadership to areas that needed their expertise and skills. To this day, they continue to communicate through email and reflect on their journey together.

> *"Never doubt that a small group of committed people can change the world. Indeed, it is the only thing that ever has."*
> —Margaret Mead, American cultural anthropologist

The world needs strong, consensus-building leaders who can focus on cross-cultural understanding in order to get a job done. This international leadership experience continually surfaces in projects with which I am currently involved. I reflect on goals and strategies I thought were perfectly stated initially, yet always seem to need revising! When it comes to international leadership, you need the flexibility to adapt to changing circumstances.

Re-evaluating the effectiveness of the leadership skills I have brought to projects, I realize how I have helped build cross-cultural bridges, trained new, local leaders and, of course, facilitated movement where needed. As technology makes the world smaller and draws everyone closer, you can have fabulous conversations and interactions around the globe. You can organize almost anything. When leading projects that extend your hopes and dreams to other cultures, remember to be culturally considerate. It is of utmost importance as you share ideas and work together to make our world a better place for everyone.

As the world gets smaller, as we get closer to each other, all we have to do is use Skype® to have fabulous conversations and see each other across the globe. We can organize almost anything. Yet, even though we have a smaller world via technology, we still need to be culturally considerate in leading projects that extend our hopes and dreams in other cultures. As the world gets smaller, reaching out gets easier. Let us share ideas and work together to make our world better for all.

LINDSAY SHIELDS
The LJ Group

*As the world gets smaller,
reaching out gets easier*

(562) 621-0521

lindsay@ljgroup.biz

www.ljgroup.biz

A global approach has always been Lindsay Shield's big picture, from her international studies at University of California, Los Angeles, to starting a foundation offering business exchanges to women in underdeveloped countries. Her objective is to serve the nonprofit community by providing skills, resources and management processes that help organizations achieve a higher level of success.

Trained in management, fundraising, event production, marketing and public relations, Lindsay devotes most of her time to the nonprofit sector. She is principal of The LJ Group, a management, fund development and events production partnership. Her clients include nonprofit organizations such as the California Arts Council,® Virginia Avenue Project® and Long Beach Cares.®

Lindsay is a graduate of the University of California, Los Angeles and an American Women's Economic Development® alumna. She serves on several boards of directors, including the Long Beach Police Foundation, and has received numerous awards, such as the American Business Women's Association® Business Associate of the Year award, the Women Who Make a Difference Award from Soroptimist International,® and the Best Facilitator honor from the International Women's Development and Promotion Association® in Beijing, China.

Everyday Leadership
Lead . . . Wherever You Are
By Christina Dyer, LCPC

Wisdom, quiet strength, decisive action and commitment to others are qualities of leadership excellence. Thousands of books, blogs and magazines on a variety of leadership topics exist today extolling the traits necessary to becoming a powerful leader.

In its infancy, leadership is born of personal power. In 1887, Lord Acton penned, "All power tends to corrupt, and absolute power corrupts absolutely." However, over time, a more compelling truth has emerged, and throughout the world, we see it is actually *powerlessness* that corrupts. A lack of individual power erodes hope and erases dreams. It saps courage to make decisions toward the betterment of ourselves, ultimately robbing society of its own *collective potential*. Stripping away autonomous power from the masses of individuals, while nurturing a dependence on the leadership of a few, has been the modus operandi for too many dictators of this past century. The economic, social and political impact of a nation of powerless people can be staggering, if not frightening in its ripple effect on the entire world. However, today there is reason to be hopeful.

More and more extraordinary leaders are emerging from the ordinary. As our world's population continues to grow, technological advances are causing our world to shrink. Our virtual interconnectedness is weaving a rich tapestry of hope that individuals joined together can raise a clamorous voice and bring effective change to our world. Leaders of governments, large corporations, powerful media empires and international philanthropic organizations are recognizing that a few powerful voices can inspire the masses to overturn a nation's leadership or raise millions of dollars after a natural disaster. Having the power or the title is not a requirement for an everyday leader. We have developed the cutting-edge tools. Now, it is in our power to undertake the personal work and develop our individual voices as leaders.

Self-Mastery

"There is nothing enlightened about shrinking so that other people won't feel insecure around you. You were born to make manifest the glory of God that is within you. It is not just in some of us . . .
It is in everyone."
—Marianne Williamson, American author, lecturer and activist

It is essential that you return to the basics and begin with yourself. What makes *you,* as an everyday leader, stand out of the crowd amidst the cacophony of voices? It begins with self-mastery.

- **Know thyself**—Do the inner work. Mastery of yourself is a process, not an event ever finished. Turn off your inner critic and give yourself the freedom to make small shifts of change—acknowledge your flaws and strengths. You cannot change what you do not acknowledge.

- **Transform thyself**—Do the outer work. Write down your commitment to your personal leadership development in all areas of your life. Sometimes, you need to *do* certain things. Often, you need to *stop doing* certain things or perhaps release something. Ask yourself, "What would move me forward more—doing or stopping?" Go from there.

- **Master thyself**—Do the daily work. Part of the art of being a powerful everyday leader lies in your ability to steadily manage your inner shifts with wisdom, grace and a sense of humor. Laughing at the outer shifts strengthens your ability to be an authentic, fully-formed woman. Examine the external factors that influence your decisions. Acknowledge them, embrace or discard them, and make peace with them.

Self-Mastery Action Step. Begin to notice the rumblings of frustration, anger or impatience in yourself and pay attention to your reaction. Decide on your ideal reaction for the next time you are faced with a situation that triggers one of these responses, and rehearse in your mind how you would rather respond. When you feel the rumblings again, take a few moments and calmly react as planned. This new self-awareness and self-control practiced repeatedly is the development of self-mastery.

Respect the Context of Your Life

You may think you are unable to swim against the tide of your current circumstances. What if you feel that your whole life is set up to sabotage all the greatness you know is within? The day-to-day taskmaster of life begins to steal away your minutes at breakfast, and ultimately eats your resolve for dinner. You collapse into bed at night exhausted and spent, taking in a morsel of satisfaction that at least those around you are satisfied and happy, content and nurtured. This is when the hard work reaps its greatest reward. *You* are the only one who can create your life. We become our choices.

Respecting the context of our lives and mastering daily challenges epitomizes everyday leadership. If you are an artist, do you give yourself one hour each day to feed your soul with poetry? If you have a stressful project at work, do you give yourself one hour after work to de-stress at the gym? These seemingly banal choices are what, in fact, make an everyday leader a great one. When you know what can be done only by you, your priorities become clear and your path opens up.

Personally, my greatest wisdom has evolved from the experience of hard choices. Leaving my young children and traveling to Africa for my nonprofit was one of the most difficult decisions of my life. Intuitively, it felt like a "must," rather than a "might." Although I was fearful, I honored my intuition. In a village in the middle of nowhere in Africa, I met a small, yet mighty, woman. *She* taught me about power and everyday leadership.

In spite of her stature and with her intense, quiet stare, she emerged as the leader of a group of twenty or so raucous, ululating women. Untitled, unknown and unimportant to the larger world, she *personified* leadership. She silently led me and a handful of other women to a small, damp, mud structure. She spoke only after we were safely out of earshot of the men in the crowd.

"I am Bibi Jeku," she declared, as she pounded her fist upon her chest, while the other women in her group nodded affirmatively.

Proud, intense and purposeful, Jeku vividly described the power-lessness of the women in this region and the limits placed on their everyday choices by the oppressive male village leaders, husbands and teenage sons. In whispered desperation, she asked for help—woman-to-woman, leader-to-leader. While others looked around nervously, afraid of being overheard by village elders, she held my gaze and spoke intently and purposefully. Then something fantastic began to happen. Her willingness to do and say what was happening in their community empowered the other women to speak. Slowly, they built their strength on the shoulders of hers—joining their voices with Jeku.

With or without titles, everyday leaders impress, influence and inspire those around them. Jeku's confessions about life for herself and her sisters in their village inspired the other women to slowly, albeit fearfully, tell me their own stories. I became overwhelmed by the hardships and injustices these women face every day. To this day, I mourn the loss of her potential for her continent and for this world. In her presence, I felt small, weak-willed and spoiled. She understood what she could accomplish with her life, and she led herself and her fellow women within that context. Her resolve strengthened my own.

I was taught one of the greatest lessons of my life—the strength of everyday leadership by a four foot, ten inch old woman.

> *"It is never too late to be what you might have been."*
> —George Eliot, British novelist

In the marathon of life, you can be many things, but not all at once. Time, place, and—for too many women—culture limits potential. Relish where you are and what you can do today, and then *do it now*. Do it for Jeku and her sisters.

Respect for Context Action Step. Pay attention to where you spend your moments now and take charge of them. Delegate mundane tasks better done by another, so you free up your time to focus on your highest priorities.

Where do *you* lead with confidence knowing no one else can do better than you can? Therein are your strengths.

Where do you feel unsure, shaky or even invisible? Therein are your opportunities for growth.

Respect the context of your life and act as if you are working with a blank canvas from this point forward. Draw, paint or sculpt—create the next phase of your journey toward your whole life's panorama. Begin now.

Sustained Motivation through Purpose and Meaning

If self-mastery is the *who,* and context is the *where,* purpose and meaning are the *why.* Being inspired and motivated to change your life can be a heady experience. You have the "get up and go," you are excited about change, and you start out with fervor and enthusiasm. Then you lose that gusto and become apathetic toward your goals and frustrated with yourself.

The truth is that this process is not easy. Everyday leadership requires you do the hard thing even when you no longer want to do it. This very act of doing what you must do is one of the hardest things in life and the hallmark of everyday leadership.

When your motivation is tied to a greater purpose, you are better able to push through problems. Challenges and adversity do not paralyze you. They chisel away the "fat" and sculpt you as a leader; they reveal your core of strength.

> *Being defeated is only a temporary condition. Giving up*
> *is what makes it permanent."*
> —Marilyn Vos Savant, American writer and columnist

Leading through this process is not a virtue—it is a choice. Everyday leaders bring clarity, focus and a sense of purpose to themselves and others. Their vision for the future is so clear to them they cannot help but inspire others to *want* to be part of something larger.

Sustained Motivation Action Step. I encourage you to create a vision statement for your life. Fill it with the people and the areas of importance to you—family, friends, colleagues, career, art, music, travel and so on.

Look at your life in its entirety including where you are currently—the context—and where you want to go and grow. Anchor your vision to reality with vivid details that lend texture and richness. Once you define what has meaning for you, you can rely on this vision statement to sustain you when you no longer have the energy, conviction and tenacity to stride toward your goals.

Courage and Commitment

I have never met anyone over the age of three who is fearless. Fear is in everyone. It is often disguised as laziness, apathy, addiction, defiance, depression—and in an overreaction to criticism or even constructive feedback—playing small and not expressing your true light. Fear shrinks your world and holds you hostage in your own safe little corner of the world. You say no to opportunities and hide behind tasks and mundane responsibilities rather than doing the bigger, more frightening challenges of life.

Whether it is a gut reaction that simply says, "I can't do that!" to full-blown panic attacks, fear is ugly, debilitating and embarrassing. Recognizing the key to unlocking the handcuffs of fear and leading yourself to freedom can be terrifying and exciting. It is a bit like free falling, yet free at the same time.

The largeness of your life is inversely proportional to fear. When fear shrinks, courage expands. To lead, you must acknowledge your fear, muster courage and march through it.

> *"Keep your fears to yourself, but share your courage with others."*
> —Robert Louis Stevenson, Scottish writer and poet

Being bold and stepping out is an act of everyday leadership. This is saying, "Yes!" when you want to scream, "No." Trust that somewhere deep inside you is a reservoir of strength and power. Commit to that. Remember Bibi Jeku—a frail, elderly woman in a village ruled by patriarchal leaders who adhere to a strict code that dealt out harsh punishments for its women. With no money, very few resources and little or no rights, she stood up for her group. Jeku was wise enough to speak in private *and* courageous enough to champion the struggle for the survival of the women of her group—for all the other frail, elderly women and for the next generation of women, for the mothers and the girls. Her voice was the voice for those who did not have the strength to speak for themselves.

Courage and Commitment Action Step. Jeku was a mentor for me. I have met no one more inspiring than she was.

Who are the inspiring people in your life?

Who shows up and stands up for their convictions every day?

Borrow their strength and courage for a moment and name your fear(s). Bring them out in the open and ask yourself:

• What would I do with my life if I were unafraid?

• What do I need to have or do to walk through this toward my goal?

• What would I gain if I were to do it? What will I lose if I do not?

Commit to yourself and those around you and become brave. When you have mastered fear, pay it forward and teach someone else to do the same. One of the best ways I know of stepping outside your own world is to help someone less fortunate do the same.

Develop an Attitude of Service and Generosity

> *"Rather than seeing the world as divided among different*
> *civilizations or classes, our collective future rests upon our*
> *embracing a vision of a single world in which we are all connected."*
> —Jacqueline Novogratz, American author, founder of Acumen Fund

The world needs everyday leadership. Our planet's most complex problems cannot be tackled or fixed by any one sector or group. Leadership that harnesses and directs the strength of the individual voice is required for our increasingly networked world. Collaborative partnerships between society, government and the private sectors stand the best chance of creating enduring solutions for the ills of today by creating a web of services that benefit all people in society. Citizens who lead their everyday lives with an attitude of service and generosity have the capacity to revolutionize the greater good more immensely than ever before. This is the nature of everyday leadership.

By virtue of our history of struggle, women have had to learn to recognize and reward our own intrinsic strength, to stand powerfully alone and to lead our lives in such a way that our voice is heard, our vote counted. Today, the term "soft power" is being used by governments to describe negotiation and diplomacy in contrast to "might and fight." Women have been utilizing soft power forever. We have always known that we are strengthened when the whole is strengthened.

Developing an Attitude of Service and Generosity Action Step. There are so many ways to share your time, expertise, money and voice. Even informing others of an organization that does good work is an act of everyday leadership through service and generosity.

• Give with your heart *and* your head. Give to good ideas that offer "handups"—not handouts. Assume strength, not fragility when working in the world.

• Join online philanthropic discussion groups and learn about the innovative ideas being examined and debated. Many fantastic collaborations are being created in the world today by everyday leaders.

"I am only one,
But still I am one.
I cannot do everything,
But still I can do something;
And because I cannot do everything
I will not refuse to do
the something that I can do."

—Helen Keller, American author, political activist and lecturer

The extraordinary resides within your ordinary, everyday life. Create enduring greatness in your life through honest self-examination, courageous acts, and sustained commitment to your best purpose. To lead from where you are, what must you do first? Is it something that will change the world or is it simply making amends with your neighbor? Is it to be kinder and more present to your parents, children, partner or best friend? Is it simply to be gentler, happier and more patient with yourself?

I challenge you to define it and begin now. Be the best not that you know how to be, but that you aspire to be. Elicit your power from within, as that is where greatness resides.

Everyday leadership requires that through authentic action we call forth the honesty, tenacity and dedication to living our best life each day. Our responsibility to the greater good and ourselves lies in our responses to these common and most personal experiences. My hope for you is to rise up, do the work, stand strong and lead in everyday moments.

CHRISTINA DYER, LCPC
Christina Dyer Consulting Services, Inc.

Inspiring Everyday Leadership

(815) 476-5600

cdyer@christinadyer.com

www.christinadyer.com

In 1997, burnt out by her career in social work, Christina Dyer radically changed the trajectory of her life and began anew. Backpacking independently through more than 25 countries, Christina spent a rich and provocative year exploring the world and photographing fascinating people in diverse cultures. This experience gave Christina a unique, compelling perspective on life and living. Her experiences gave her the passion to embrace global leadership development. She has worked with corporate America, government agencies and has led two international nonprofits serving in Africa.

Christina holds a master's degree in counseling psychology and is a licensed clinical professional counselor. She has been interviewed for radio and newspapers around the world and was featured for her exemplary social service on CBS News Magazine's *48 Hours with Dan Rather.*

Today, Christina runs her own company as a leadership development consultant, personal and corporate coach and professional speaker. She brings her education, diverse career experiences and passion for life's adventures to her consulting work. She teaches leaders to influence others to take action; inspire individuals to create larger, more courageous visions for their lives; and coaches teams to employ simple, everyday strategies to lead . . . wherever they are.

More Savvy *Leadership Strategies* for Women

Now that you have learned many things about how to become a savvy leader using a wide variety of tips, techniques and strategies, the next step is to take action. Get started applying what you have learned in the pages of this book.

We want you to know that we are here to help you meet your professional and personal objectives. What follows is a list of where we are geographically located. Regardless of where our companies are located, many of us provide a variety of services over the phone or through webinars, and we welcome the opportunity to travel to your location.

You can find out more about each of us by reading our bios at the end of our chapters, or by visiting our websites listed on the next pages. When you are ready for one-on-one consulting or group training from any of the co-authors in this book—we are available! If you call us and let us know you have read our book, we will provide you with a free phone consultation to determine your needs and how we can best serve you.

Alabama

Malena Cunningham   www.strategicmediarelationsinc.com

California

Elizabeth Agnew	www.integrative-leadership.com
Karen Báez	www.karenbaez.com
Terry Barton	www.thebartongrp.com
Karen Buckley	www.thewisdomconnection.com
Fay Freed	www.starconsulting.org
Ann Kelley	www.mbdtraining.com
Caterina Rando	www.caterinarando.com
Lindsay Shields	www.ljgroup.biz
LaNell Silverstein	www.lanellsilverstein.com
Karen Solomon	www.successapppeal.com
Kim Zilliox	www.kzleadership.com

Connecticut

Carolyn Phillips   www.fitbehavior.com

Georgia

Carla Wellington   www.visioncommgroup.com

Illinois

Christina Dyer   www.christinadyer.com

Massachusetts

Carole Sacino   www.turningpointinstitute.com

Minnesota

Jan McDonough   www.attitudeadventures.com

Jane Morrison   www.janemorrison.com

Nevada

Laura Rubeli   www.laurarubeli.com

Oregon

Marci Nemhauser   www.professionalgrowthservices.com

Also from
THRIVE Publishing™

For more information
on this book, visit
www.connectionscountbook.com

For more information
on this book, visit
www.execetiquette.com

For more information
on this book, visit
www.directsellingbook.com

For more information
on this book, visit
www.getorganizedtodaybook.com

Also from
THRIVE Publishing™

For more information
on this book, visit
www.incrediblebusinessbook.com

For more information
on this book, visit
www.mystylemywaybook.com

For more information
on this book, visit
www.momentrepreneurbook.com

For more information
on this book, visit
www.powerofcivilitybook.com

THRIVE Publishing develops books for experts who want to share their knowledge with more and more people. We provide our co-authors with a proven system, professional guidance and support, producing quality, multi-author, how-to books that uplift and enhance the personal and professional lives of the people they serve.

We know that getting a book written and published is a huge undertaking. To make that process as easy as possible, we have an experienced team with the resources and know-how to put a quality, informative book in the hands of our co-authors quickly and affordably. Our co-authors are proud to be included in THRIVE Publishing books because these publications enhance their business missions, give them a professional outreach tool and enable them to communicate essential information to a wider audience.

You can find out more about our upcoming book projects at
www.thrivebooks.com

For more copies of this book, *Savvy Leadership Strategies for Women,* contact any of the co-authors or visit
www.savvyleadershipbook.com